The Object-Oriented Thought Process

Matt Weisfeld

A Division of Macmillan USA
201 West 103rd Street, Indianapolis, Indiana, 46290

Copyright © 2000 by Sams Publishing

International Standard Book Number: 0-672-31853-9

Library of Congress Catalog Card Number: 99-066894

Printed in the United States of America

First Printing: April 2000

03   02   01   00   4   3   2   1

Trademarks

Warning and Disclaimer

ASSOCIATE PUBLISHER
Michael Stephens

ACQUISITIONS EDITOR
Steve Anglin

DEVELOPMENT EDITOR
Laura N. Williams

MANAGING EDITOR
Lisa Wilson

PROJECT EDITOR
Carol Bowers

COPY EDITOR
Kitty Jarrett

INDEXER
Sheila Schroeder

PROOFREADERS
Bob LaRoche
Jill Mazurczyk

TECHNICAL EDITOR
Charles Ashbacher

TECHNICAL REVIEWERS
Charles Ashbacher
Wolfgang Haerle

TEAM COORDINATOR
Karen Opal

MEDIA DEVELOPER
Jason Haines

INTERIOR DESIGNER
Anne Jones

COVER DESIGNER
Anne Jones

COPY WRITER
Eric Borgert

LAYOUT TECHNICIANS
Ayanna Lacey
Mark Walchle

Overview

Contents

About the Author

Matt Weisfeld is vice president of Product Development for preEmptive Solutions, a leading Java technologies company in Cleveland, Ohio. He has more than 19 years of software development, project management, and teaching experience. Matt currently teaches at Cleveland State University and holds an MS in computer science, as well as an MBA in project management. Over the past several years, Matt has published two other computer books and more than a dozen articles in magazines and journals such as *Dr. Dobb's Journal*, *The C/C++ Users Journal*, *Software Development*, *Java Report*, and the international journal *Project Management*.

About the Technical Editors and Reviewers

Charles Ashbacher has been programming for nearly 20 years, which makes him experienced and well rounded rather than old and cynical. He is coeditor of the *Journal of Recreational Mathematics* and a regular contributor to the *Journal of Object-Oriented Programming*. Charles teaches computing at all levels—corporate training, college, and community education—and his background also includes stints writing commercial code and software to conduct scientific research. He is president and CEO of Charles Ashbacher Technologies (www.ashbacher.com).

Wolfgang Haerle, Ph.D., has more than seven years of hands-on SAP experience, with lead technical knowledge in the areas of SAP R/3 system administration and tuning; the ABAP/4 Development Workbench Correction & Transport System; SAPscript; CPIC/RFC; Workflow; ALE/EDI fax solutions; and Web@Studio, ITS, and ABAP objects. Dr. Haerle also has functional knowledge in the areas of SD, MM, and FI, and has been awarded membership in International Who's Who, in the information technology category.

Dedication

To Bram.

Acknowledgments

This book required the effort and assistance of many people. I would like to take the time to acknowledge as many of these people as possible, for without them, this book would never have happened.

First and foremost, I would like to thank my wife, Sharon, for all her help. Not only did she provide support and encouragement throughout this lengthy process, but she edited every chapter of the initial draft.

As always, I would like to thank my parents for their continued support in everything that I do.

The people I worked with at Sams Publishing are really first rate. Thanks to Tim Ryan for working with me to make the book a reality. I would like to express my appreciation to Charles Ashbacher, who did a thorough tech edit of the first draft. Charles Ashbacher and Wolfgang Haerle both did a fine job with the technical review and thanks to Kitty Jarrett for her work as the copy editor. Thanks as well to Karen Opal, the team coordinator, with whom I made first contact at Sams and who has helped me throughout this process and Carol Bowers who handled the production editing. Special thanks to the development editor, Laura Williams, who not only did a great job editing, but was able to keep me focused as well.

Thanks to my friends Gabe Torok, Paul Tyma, and Jim Gross, who reviewed various parts of the manuscripts and helped me immensely with technical questions and other philosophical issues. And thanks to Todd Weisfeld, Dan Pigford, and Bryan Hutchinson for helping me with the object-oriented courseware that inspired this book.

Finally, thanks to my daughters, Stacy and Stephanie, who, as always, keep me on my toes and to my cat, Samson, who hung out with me during most of the seemingly endless hours that I spent writing and editing the manuscript.

Tell Us What You Think!

As the reader of this book, *you* are our most important critic and commentator. We value your opinion and want to know what we're doing right, what we could do better, in what areas you'd like to see us publish, and any other words of wisdom you're willing to pass our way.

As an associate publisher for Sams Publishing, I welcome your comments. You can fax, email, or write me directly to let me know what you do or don't like about this book—as well as what we can do to make our books stronger.

Please note that I cannot help you with technical problems related to the topic of this book, and that due to the high volume of mail I receive, I might not be able to reply to every message.

When you write, please be sure to include this book's title and author as well as your name and phone or fax number. I will carefully review your comments and share them with the author and editors who worked on the book.

Fax: 317-581-4770

Email: Michael.Stephens@macmillanusa.com

Mail: Michael Stephens
         Sams Publishing
         201 West 103rd Street
         Indianapolis, IN 46290 USA

Foreword

Several decades ago, when I learned to write software, programs were not object oriented. Today, almost every significant program uses objects. Nevertheless, many modern programs are not truly object oriented because many—perhaps most—modern programmers do not fully comprehend the object-oriented paradigm. Objects, although now ubiquitous, are poorly understood.

Objects are poorly understood at least in part because they *are* ubiquitous. Almost a millenium ago, Pliny the Younger observed how we become inattentive to the commonplace: "Objects...are often overlooked and neglected if they lie under our eye" (Letter xx. 1). Although Pliny obviously had in mind real-world objects, not software objects, his point is equally true of software objects.

Therefore, programmers who aim to create high-quality software—as all programmers should—must learn the varied subtleties of the familiar yet not-so-familiar beasts called *objects* and *classes*. Doing so entails careful study of books such as this one. Beginners and veterans alike can benefit from attending to what the author correctly sees as foundational: how to think in an object-oriented manner.

So, as the voice heard by St. Augustine of Hippo said, "Take up and read." (*Confessions*, Book IIX, Chapter 12, Verse 29) And after you've done so, do it again. The users of your software will be glad you did.

Bill McCarty

La Habra, California

December 1999

Introduction

This Book's Scope

As the title suggests, this book is about the object-oriented (O-O) thought process. Obviously, choosing the theme and title of the book are important decisions; however, these decisions were not all that simple. Numerous books deal with one level or another of object orientation. Several popular books deal with topics including O-O analysis, O-O design, O-O programming, design patterns, O-O databases, the Unified Modeling Language (UML), various O-O programming languages, and many other topics related to O-O programming.

However, while poring over all these books, many people forget that all these topics are built on a single foundation: how you think in O-O ways. It is unfortunate, but often software professionals dive into these books without taking the appropriate time and effort to *really* understand the concepts in them.

I contend that learning O-O concepts is not accomplished by learning a specific development method or a set of tools. Doing things in an O-O manner is, simply put, a way of thinking. This book is all about the O-O thought process.

Separating the methods and tools from the O-O thought process is not easy. Many people are introduced to O-O concepts via one of these methods or tools. Many C programmers were first introduced to object orientation by migrating to C++—before they were even exposed directly to O-O concepts. Some software professionals were first introduced to object orientation by presentations that included object models using UML—again, before they were even exposed directly to O-O concepts.

It is important to understand the significant difference between learning O-O concepts and using the methods and tools that support the paradigm. In his article "What the UML Is—and Isn't," Craig Larman states, "Unfortunately, in the context of software engineering and the UML diagramming language, acquiring the skills to read and write UML notation seems to sometimes be equated with skill in object-oriented analysis and design. Of course, this is not so, and the latter is much more important than the former. Therefore, I recommend seeking education and educational materials in which intellectual skill in object-oriented analysis and design is paramount rather than UML notation or the use of a case tool."

Although learning a modeling language is an important step, it is much more important to learn O-O skills first. Learning UML before O-O concepts is similar to learning how to read an electrical diagram without first knowing anything about electricity.

The same problem occurs with programming languages. As stated earlier, many C programmers moved into the realm of object orientation by migrating to C++ before being directly exposed to O-O concepts. Many times developers who claim to be C++ programmers are simply C programmers using C++ compilers.

C++ was a major milestone in the history of computer programming languages. It continues to be a primary force in the programming language market. Despite the fact that C++ is one of the most powerful programming tools available today, it is a descendent of the C programming language, which causes some problems. C is not O-O, and C++ was developed to be backward compatible with C. In this way, it is quite possible to use a C++ compiler with C syntax and forsake all of C++'s O-O features. Even worse, a programmer can use just enough O-O features to make a program incomprehensible to O-O and non-O-O programmers alike.

Thus, it is of vital importance that while you're on the road to O-O development, you first learn the fundamental O-O concepts. Resist the temptation to jump directly into a programming language (such as C++ or Java) or a modeling language (such as UML), and take the time to learn the object-oriented thought process.

In my first class in Smalltalk in the late 1980s, the instructor told the class that the new O-O paradigm was a totally new way of thinking. He went on to say that although all of us were most likely very good programmers, about 10%–20% of us would never really grasp the O-O way of doing things. If this statement is indeed true, it is most likely because some people never really take the time to make the paradigm shift and learn the underlying O-O concepts.

The Intended Audience

This book is a general introduction to fundamental O-O concepts. The intended audience includes designers, developers, project managers, and anyone who wants to gain a general understanding of what object orientation is all about. Reading this book should provide a strong foundation for moving to other books covering more advanced O-O topics.

Of these more advanced books, one of my favorites is *Object-Oriented Design in Java* by Stephen Gilbert and Bill McCarty. I really like the approach of the book and have used it as a textbook in classes I have taught on O-O concepts. I cite *Object-Oriented Design in Java* often throughout this book, and I recommend that you graduate to it after you complete this one.

Other books that I have found very helpful include *Effective C++* by Scott Meyers, *Classical and Object-Oriented Software Engineering* by Stephen R. Schach, *Thinking in C++* by Bruce Eckel, *UML Distilled* by Martin Flower, and *Java Design* by Peter Coad and Mark Mayfield.

While teaching intro-level Java to programmers at corporations and universities, it quickly became obvious to me that most of these programmers easily picked up the Java syntax. However, these same programmers struggled with the O-O nature of the language.

This Book's Scope

It should be obvious by now that I am a firm believer in becoming comfortable with the object-oriented thought process before jumping into a programming language or modeling language. This book is filled with examples of Java code and UML diagrams; however, you do not need to know Java or UML to read this book. After all I have said about learning the concepts first, why is there so much Java code and so many UML diagrams in this book? First, they are both great for illustrating O-O concepts. Second, both are vital to the O-O process and should be addressed at an introductory level. The key is not to focus on Java or UML, but to use them as aids in the understanding of the underlying concepts.

Appendix A, "An Overview of UML Used in This Book," explains the UML notation used in this book.

The Java examples in the book illustrate concepts such as loops and functions. However, understanding the code itself is not a prerequisite for understanding the concepts, but, it might be helpful to have a book at hand that covers Java syntax.

I cannot state too strongly that this book does *not* teach Java or UML, both of which can command volumes unto themselves. It is my hope that this book will whet your appetite for other O-O topics such as O-O analysis, object-oriented design, and O-O programming.

Happy object hunting!

References and Suggested Reading

Coad, Peter, and Mark Mayfield: *Java Design*. Object International, 1999.

Eckel, Bruce: *Thinking in C++*. Prentice Hall, 1995.

Flower, Martin: *UML Distilled*. Addison Wesley Longman, 1997.

Gilbert, Stephen, and Bill McCarty: *Object-Oriented Design in Java*. The Waite Group, 1998.

Khoshafian, Setrag, and Razmik Abnous: *Object Orientation*. Wiley, 1995.

Larman, Craig: "What the UML Is—and Isn't," *Java Report*, volume 4 (issue 5): pages 20-24, May, 1999.

Meyers, Scott: *Effective C++*. Addison-Wesley, 1992.

Schach, Stephen R.: *Classical and Object-Oriented Software Engineering*. Irwin, 1996.

Tyma, Paul, Gabriel Torok and Troy Downing: *Java Primer Plus*. The Waite Group, 1996.

Introduction to Object-Oriented Concepts

IN THIS CHAPTER

- **Learn what an object really is**
- **Learn what a class really is**
- **Understand the difference between an object and a class**
- **Learn the fundamental object-oriented concepts**

Object-oriented (O-O) software development has been around since the early 1960s. Yet today, most software shops are not primarily O-O. It is no secret that the software industry can be slow moving at times. It is also true that, when working systems are in place, there has to be a compelling reason to replace them. This has hindered the propagation of O-O systems. There are a lot of non-O-O, *legacy systems* (that is, older systems that are already in place) that seem to be working just fine—so why risk potential disaster by changing them? In most cases you should not change them, at least not simply for the sake of change. There is nothing inherently wrong with systems written in non–O-O code. However, brand-new development definitely warrants consideration of using O-O technologies.

Although there has been a steady and significant growth in O-O development in the past 10 years, an entirely new venue has helped catapult it more into the mainstream. The emergence of the Web has opened a brand-new arena, where much of the software development is new and mostly unencumbered by legacy concerns. Even when there are legacy concerns, there is a trend to wrap the legacy systems in object wrappers.

Objects are slowly but surely making their way into our professional information systems (IS) lives—and they cannot be ignored. In products such as PowerBuilder to Visual Basic, objects are becoming a major part of the IS equation. With the explosion of the Internet and Java, the electronic highway is really becoming an object-based highway. And as businesses gravitate toward the Web, they are gravitating toward objects because the technologies used for the Web are mostly O-O in nature.

This chapter is an overview of the fundamental O-O concepts. The topics covered in this chapter touch on most, if not all, of the topics covered in subsequent chapters, which explore the issues in much greater detail.

Procedural Versus O-O Programming

What is all the fuss about objects? There are many reasons O-O evangelists believe the industry should shift toward objects. Perhaps the most often-cited advantage is code reuse. A burgeoning software component industry, in theory, allows software developers the advantage of using previously built and tested code so that they do not have to reinvent the wheel. The topic of code reuse is covered at length throughout this book, particularly in Chapter 8, "Frameworks and Reuse: Designing with Interfaces and Abstract Classes."

Before we delve deeper into the advantages of O-O development, let's consider a more fundamental question: What exactly is an object? This is both a complex and a simple question. It is complex because shifting gears to learn a totally new way of thinking is not an easy task. It is simple in the sense that most people already think in terms of objects.

For example, when you look at a person, you see the person as an object. The person has attributes, such as eye color, behavior, and a certain way of walking. In its basic definition, an object is an entity that contains both data and behavior. This is the key difference between the more traditional programming methodology, procedural programming, and O-O programming. In procedural programming, code is placed into functions or procedures. Ideally, as shown in Figure 1.1, these procedures then become "black boxes," where inputs come in and outputs come out. Data is placed into separate structures, and is manipulated by these functions or procedures.

FIGURE 1.1
Black boxes.

Procedural programming has been the mainstay since the Bronze Age of computers—so why change? First, as illustrated in Figure 1.2, in procedural programming the data is separated from the procedures, and often the data is global, so it is easy to modify data that is outside your scope. This means that access to data is uncontrolled and unpredictable. Second, because you have no control over who has access to the data, testing and debugging are much more difficult.

Objects address these problems by combining data and behavior into a nice, complete package. Objects are not just primitive data types, like integers and strings. Objects do contain entities such as integers and strings, but they also contain methods (in O-O terminology, functions are called *methods*) that you can use to operate on the data types. You can also control access to members of an object. This means that some members, such as data types and methods, can be hidden from other objects. For instance, an object called Math may contain two integers, called myInt1 and myInt2. Most likely, the Math object also contains the necessary methods to set and retrieve the values of myInt1 and myInt2. It may also contain a method called Sum() to add the two integers together.

By combining the data and methods in the same entity, which in O-O parlance is called *encapsulation*, we can control access to the data in the Math object. By defining these integers as off-limits, another, logically unconnected, function cannot manipulate the integers myInt1 and myInt2—only the Math object can do that.

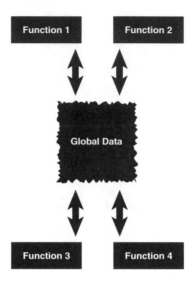

FIGURE 1.2
Using global data.

WARNING

Keep in mind that it is possible to create poorly designed classes that do not restrict access to class attributes. The bottom line is that you can design bad code just as efficiently with O-O design as with any other programming methodology. Simply take care to adhere to sound class design guidelines.

What happens when another object—for example, myObject—wants to gain access to the sum of myInt1 and myInt2? It asks the Math object: myObject sends a message to the Math object. Figure 1.3 shows how the two objects communicate with each other via their methods. The message is really a call to the Math object's Sum method. The Sum method then returns the value to myObject. The beauty of this is that myObject does not need to know how the sum is calculated (although I'm sure it can guess). In this example, you can change how the Math object calculates the sum without making a change to myObject (as long as the means to retrieve the sum do not change). All you want is the sum—you don't care how it is calculated.

Calculating the sum is not the responsibility of myObject—it is the Math object's responsibility. As long as myObject has access to the Math object, it can send the appropriate message and then obtain the result. In general, objects should not manipulate the internal data of other objects (that is, myObject should not directly change the value of myInt1 and myInt2). In most cases it is better to build small objects with specific tasks than to build large objects with many tasks and more complex data and methods.

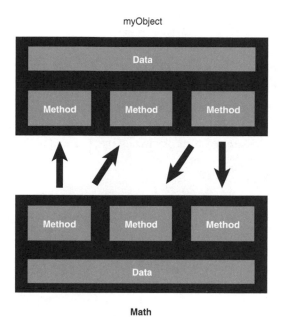

FIGURE 1.3
Object-to-object communication.

What Makes O-O Different from Procedural Programming?

Now that we have a general understanding about some of the differences about procedural and object-oriented technologies, let's delve deeper into both.

Procedural Programming

Procedural programming separates the data of the program from the operations that manipulate the data. For example, if you want to send information across a network, only the relevant data is sent (see Figure 1.4), with the expectation that the program at the other end of the pipe knows what to do with it.

FIGURE 1.4
Data transmitted over a wire.

O-O Programming

The fundamental advantage of O-O programming is that the data and the operations that manipulate the data are both contained in the object. For example, when an object is transported across a network, the entire object, including the data and behavior, goes with it. In Figure 1.5, the `Employee` object is sent over the network.

FIGURE 1.5
Objects transmitted over a wire.

What Exactly Is an Object?

Objects are the building blocks of an O-O program. A program that uses O-O technology is basically a collection of objects. To illustrate, let's consider that a corporate system contains objects that represent employees of that company. Each of these objects is made up of the data and behavior described in the following sections.

Object Data

The data stored within an object represents the *state* of the object. In O-O programming terminology, this data is called *attributes*. In our example, as shown in Figure 1.6, employee attributes could be Social Security numbers, date of birth, gender, phone number, etc. The attributes contain the information that differentiates between the various objects, in this case the employees. Attributes are covered in more detail later in this chapter in the discussion on classes.

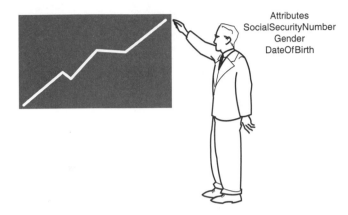

FIGURE 1.6
Employee attributes.

Object Behaviors

The *behavior* of an object is what the object can do. In procedural languages the behavior is
defined by procedures, functions, and subroutines. In O-O programming terminology these
behaviors are contained in *methods,* and you invoke a method by sending a *message* to it. In
our employee example, consider that one of the behaviors required of an employee object is to
set and return the values of the various attributes. Thus, each attribute would have corresponding methods, such as setGender() and getGender(). In this case, when another object needs
this information, it can send a message to an employee object and ask it what its gender is.

Note that we are only showing the interface of the methods, and not the implementation. The
following is all the user needs to know to effectively use the methods:

- The name of the method
- The parameters passed to the method
- The return type of the method

To further illustrate behaviors, consider Figure 1.7.

In Figure 1.7, the Payroll object contains a method called CalculatePay() that calculates the
pay for a specific employee. Among other information, the Payroll object must obtain the
Social Security number of this employee. To get this information, the payroll object must send
a message to the Employee object (in this case, the getSocialSecurityNumber() method). The
employee object recognizes the message and returns the requested information.

Employee Object

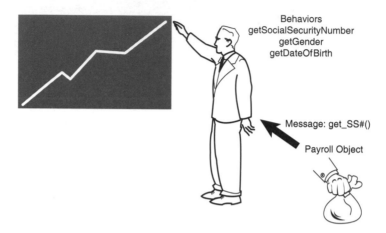

Behaviors
getSocialSecurityNumber
getGender
getDateOfBirth

Message: get_SS#()

Payroll Object

FIGURE 1.7
Employee behaviors.

To illustrate further, Figure 1.8 is a class diagram representing the `Employee/Payroll` system we have been talking about.

TIP

UML Class Diagrams

Note that because this is the first class diagram we have seen, it is very basic and lacks some of the constructs (such as constructors) that a proper class should contain. Fear not—we will discuss class diagrams and constructors in more detail in Chapter 3, "Advanced Object-Oriented Concepts."

Each class diagram is broken up into two separate sections (besides the name itself). The first section contains the data (attributes), and the second section contains the behaviors (methods). In Figure 1.8, the `Employee` class diagram's attribute section contains `SocialSecurityNumber`, `Gender` and `DateofBirth`, while the method section contains the methods that operate on these attributes. You can use programming tools such as TogetherJ, to create and maintain class diagrams that correspond to real code.

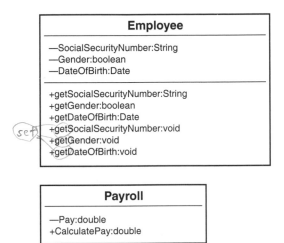

FIGURE 1.8

Employee and payroll class diagrams.

TIP

Modeling Tools

TogetherJ is a visual modeling tool that provides a mechanism to create and manipulate class diagrams using the Unified Modeling Language (UML). UML is discussed throughout this book, and you can find a tutorial on its notation in Appendix A, "An Overview of UML Used in This Book."

We will get into the relationships between classes and objects later in this chapter, but for now you can think of a class as a template from which objects are made. When an object is created, we say that the objects are *instantiated*. Thus, if we create three employees, we are actually creating three instances of an Employee class. Each object contains its own copy of the attributes and methods. For example, consider Figure 1.9. An employee object called John (John is its identity) has its own copy of all the attributes and methods defined in the Employee class. An employee object called Mary has its own copy of attributes and methods. They both have a separate copy of the DateOfBirth attribute and the getDateOfBirth method.

Program Space

// Data-attributes
SocialSecurityNumber;
Gender;
DateOfBirth;

// Behavior-methods
getSocialSecurityNumber() {}
getGender() {}
getDateOfBirth() {}
getSocialSecurityNumber(){}
getGender() {}
getDateOfBirth() {}

Reference: John

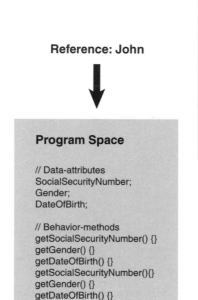

Program Space

// Data-attributes
SocialSecurityNumber;
Gender;
DateOfBirth;

// Behavior-methods
getSocialSecurityNumber() {}
getGender() {}
getDateOfBirth() {}
getSocialSecurityNumber(){}
getGender() {}
getDateOfBirth() {}

Reference: Mary

FIGURE 1.9
Program spaces.

WARNING

Be aware that there is not a physical copy of each method for each object. Rather, each object points to the same physical code. However, this is an implementation issue left up to the compiler/operating platform. From a conceptual level, you can think of objects as being wholly independent and having their own attributes and methods.

What Exactly Is a Class?

In short, a *class* is a blueprint for an object. When you instantiate an object, you use a class as the basis for how the object is built. In fact, trying to explain classes and objects is really a chicken-and-egg dilemma. It is difficult to describe a class without using the term *object*, and to describe an object without using the term *class*. For example, a bike is an object.

However, someone had to have the blueprints (that is, the class) to build the bike. In O-O software, unlike the chicken-and-egg dilemma, we do know what comes first—the class. An object cannot be instantiated without a class. Thus, many of the concepts in this section are similar to those presented earlier in the chapter, especially when we talk about attributes and methods.

In order to explain classes and methods, it is helpful to use an example from the relational database world. In a database table, the definition of the table itself (fields, description, and data types used) would be a class (metadata), and the objects would be the rows of the table (data)

This book focuses on the concepts of O-O software, and not on a specific implementation (such as Java, C++, or Smalltalk), but it is often helpful to use code examples to explain some concepts, so Java code fragments are used to help explain some concepts when appropriate. The following sections describe some of the fundamental concepts of classes and how they interact.

Classes Are Object Templates

Classes can be thought of as the templates, or cookie cutters, for objects as seen in Figure 1.10. A class is used to create an object.

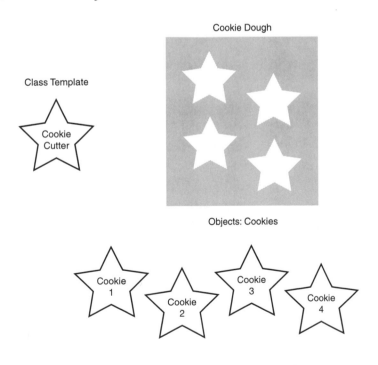

FIGURE 1.10
Class template.

A class can be thought of as a sort of higher-level data type. For example, just as you create an integer or a float:

```
int x;
float y;
```

you create an object by using a predefined class:

```
myClass myObject;
```

Because of the names used in this example, it is obvious that `myClass` is the class and `myObject` is the object.

Remember that each object has its own attributes (analogous to fields) and behaviors (analogous to functions or routines). A class defines the attributes and behaviors that all objects created with this class will possess. Classes are standalone components and can be distributed individually or as part of a library. Because objects are created from classes, it follows that classes must define the basic building blocks of objects (data, behavior, and messages). In short, you must design a class before you can create an object.

For example, here is a definition of a `Person` class:

```
public class Person{

    private String name, address;

    public String getName(){
        return name;
    }
    public void setName(String n){
        name = n;
    }

    public String getAddress(){
        return address;
    }
    public void setAddress(String adr){
        address = adr;
    }

}
```

Attributes

As you already saw, the data of a class is represented by attributes. Each class must define the attributes that will store the state of each object instantiated from that class. In the `Person` class example in the previous section, the `Person` class defines attributes for `name` and `address`.

> **TIP**
>
> **Access Designations**
>
> When a data type or method is defined as `public`, other objects can directly access it. When a data type or method is defined as `private`, only that specific object can access it. Another access modifier, `protected`, allows access by related objects, which you'll learn about in Chapter 3, "Advanced Object-Oriented Concepts."

Methods

As learned earlier in the chapter, methods implement the required behavior of a class. Every object instantiated from this class has these methods. Methods may implement behaviors that are called from other objects (for example, messages) or provide internal behavior of the class. Internal behaviors are methods that are not accessible by other objects (for example, private methods). In the earlier `Person` example, the behaviors are `getName()`, `setName()`, `getAddress()`, and `setAddress()`. These methods allow other objects to inspect and change the values of the object's attributes. This is common design in O-O systems. In most cases, access to attributes within an object should be controlled by the object—no object should directly change an attribute of another.

Messages

Messages are the communication mechanism between objects. For example, when Object A invokes a method of Object B, Object A is sending a message to Object B. Object B's response is defined by its return value. Only the public methods, not the private methods, of an object can be invoked by another object. The following code illustrates this concept:

```
public class Payroll{

    String name;

    Person P = new Person();

    String = P.setName("Joe");

    ... code

    String = P.getName();

}
```

In this example (assuming that a `Payroll` object is instantiated), the `Payroll` object is sending a message to a `Person` object, with the purpose of retrieving the name via the `getName` method. (Again, don't worry too much about the actual code, as we are really interested in the concepts.)

Using UML to Model a Class Diagram

Over the years many tools and models have been developed to assist in designing classes. One of the most popular today is UML. Although it is beyond the scope of this book to describe UML in fine detail, we will use UML class diagrams to illustrate the classes that we build. In fact, we have already used a class diagram in this chapter. Figure 1.11 shows the `Person` class diagram we discussed earlier in the chapter.

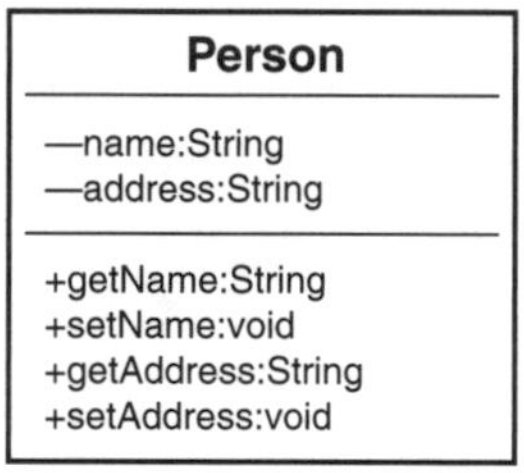

```
               Person

          —name:String
          —address:String

          +getName:String
          +setName:void
          +getAddress:String
          +setAddress:void
```

FIGURE 1.11
The person class diagram.

Again, notice that the attributes and methods are separated (the attributes on the top, and the methods on the bottom). As we delve more deeply into O-O design, these class diagrams will get much more sophisticated and convey much more information on how the different classes interact with each other.

Encapsulation

One of the primary advantages of using objects is that the object need not reveal all its attributes and behaviors. In good O-O design (at least what is generally accepted as good), an object should only reveal the interfaces needed to interact with it. Details not pertinent to the use of the object should be hidden from other objects. This is called *encapsulation*. For example, an object that calculates the square of a number must provide an interface to obtain the result. However, the internal attributes and algorithms used to calculate the square need not be made available to the requesting object. Robust classes are designed with encapsulation in mind. In the next sections, we cover the concepts of interface and implementation which are the basis of encapsulation.

Interfaces

As discussed earlier in this chapter, the interface is the fundamental means of communication between objects. Each class design specifies the interfaces for the proper instantiation and operation of objects. Any behavior that the object provides must be invoked by a message sent using one of the provided interfaces. The interface should completely describe how users of the class interact with the class. In Java, the methods that are part of the interface are designated as `public`.

Let's look at the example just mentioned: calculating the square of a number. In this example, the interface would consists of two pieces:

- How to instantiate a `Square` object
- How to send a value to the object and get the square of that value in return

Interfaces do not normally include attributes—only methods. As discussed earlier in the chapter, if a user needs access to an attribute, then a method is created to return the attribute. If a user wants the value of an attribute, a method is called that returns the value of the attribute. In this way, the attribute is encapsulated in the object, and only the object itself can change it, or even inspect it. This is of vital importance, especially in testing. If you control the access to the attribute, when a problem arises, you do not have to worry about tracking down every piece of code that may have changed the attribute.

Implementations

Only the public attributes and methods are considered the interface. The user should not see any part of the implementation—interacting with an object solely through interfaces. In the previous example, for instance the `Employee` class, only the attributes were hidden. In many cases, there will be methods that also should be hidden and thus not part of the interface. Continuing the example of the square root from the previous section, the user does not care how the square root is calculated—as long as it is the correct answer. Thus, the implementation can change and it will not affect the user's code.

A Real-World Example of the Interface/Implementation Paradigm

Figure 1.12 illustrates the interface/implementation paradigm, using real-world objects rather than code. The toaster obviously requires electricity. To get this electricity, the cord from the toaster must be plugged into the electrical outlet, which is the interface. All the toaster needs to do to get the required electricity is to use a cord that complies with the electrical outlet specifications; this is the interface between the toaster and the electricity. The fact that the actual implementation is a coal-powered electric plant is not the concern of the toaster. In fact, for all the toaster cares, the implementation could be a nuclear power plant or a local power generator. With this model, any appliance can get electricity, as long as it conforms to the interface specification as seen in Figure 1.12.

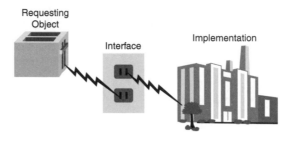

FIGURE 1.12
Power Plant Example.

A Java Example of the Interface/Implementation Paradigm

Let's explore the Square class further. Assume that you are writing a class that calculates the squares of integers. You must provide a separate interface and implementation. That is, you must provide a way for the user to invoke and obtain the square value. You must also provide the implementation that calculates the square; however, the user should not know anything about the specific implementation. Figure 1.13 shows one way to do this. Note that in the class diagram, the plus sign (+) designates public and the minus sign (-) designates private. Thus, you can identify the interface by the methods, prefaced with plus signs.

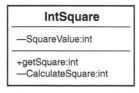

FIGURE 1.13
The square class.

This class diagram corresponds to the following code:

```
public class IntSquare {

    // private attribute
    private int SquareValue;
```

```
// public interface
public int getSquare (int value) {

    SquareValue =calculateSquare(value);

    return SquareValue;

}

// private implementation
private int calculateSquare (int value) {

    return value*value;

}
}
```

Note that the only part of the class that the user has access to is the public method getSquare, which is the interface. The implementation of the square algorithm is in the method calculateSquare, which is private. Also notice that the attribute SquareValue is private because users do not need to know that this method exists. Therefore, we have applied encapsulation to the implementation: The object only reveals the interfaces the user needs in order to interact with it, and details that are not pertinent to the use of the object are hidden from other objects.

If the implementation were to change—say, you wanted to use Java's built-in square function—you would not need to change the interface. The user would get the same functionality, but the implementation would be different changed. This is very important when you're writing code that deals with data; for example, you can move data from a file to a database without forcing the user to change any code.

Inheritance

As mentioned earlier in this chapter, one of the most powerful attributes of O-O programming is code reuse. Procedural programming provides code reuse to a certain degree—you can write a procedure and then use it as many times as you want. However, O-O programming goes an important step further, allowing you to define relationships between classes that facilitate not only code reuse, but better overall design, by organizing classes and factoring in commonalties of various classes. Inheritance is the primary means of providing this functionality.

Inheritance allows a class to inherit the attributes and methods of another class. This allows you to create brand new classes by abstracting out common attributes and behaviors.

One of the major design issues in O-O programming is to factor out commonality of the various classes. For example, say you have a `Dog` class and a `Cat` class, and each will have an attribute for eye color. In a procedural model, the code for `Dog` and `Cat` would each contain this attribute. In an O-O design, the color attribute could be abstracted up to a class called `Mammal`—along with any other common attributes and methods. In this case, both `Dog` and `Cat` inherit from the `Mammal` class, as shown in Figure 1.14.

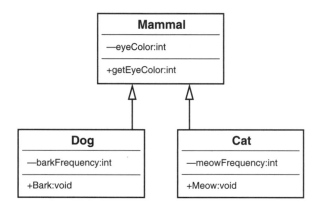

Figure 1.14
Mammal hierarchy.

The `Dog` and `Cat` classes both inherit from `Mammal`. This means that a `Dog` class actually has the following attributes:

```
eyeColor          // inherited from Mammal
barkFrequency     // defined only for Dogs
```

In the same vein, `Dog` object has the following methods:

```
GetEyeColor       // inherited from Mammal
Bark              // defined only for Dogs
```

When the `Dog` or the `Cat` object is instantiated, it contains everything in its class, as well as everything from the parent class. Thus, `Dog` has all the properties of its class definition, as well as the properties inherited from the `Mammal` class.

Superclasses and Subclasses

The superclass, or parent class, contains all the attributes and behaviors that are common to classes that inherit from it. For example, in the case of the `Mammal` class, all mammals have similar attributes such as `WarmBlooded` and `HasHair`, and behaviors such as `GenerateInternalHeat` and `GrowHair`. All mammals have these attributes and behaviors, so it is not necessary to duplicate them down the inheritance tree for each type of mammal. Thus, the Dog and Cat classes inherit all those common attributes and behaviors from the Mammal class. The Mammal class is considered the superclass of the Dog and the Cat subclasses, or child classes.

Inheritance provides a rich set of design advantages. When you're designing a Cat class, the Mammal class provides much of the functionality needed. By inheriting from the Mammal object, Cat already has all the attributes and behaviors that make it a true mammal. To make it more specifically a cat type of mammal, the Cat class must include any attributes or behaviors that pertain solely to a cat.

Abstraction

An inheritance tree can grow quite large. When the Mammal and Cat classes are complete, other mammals, such as dogs (or lions and tigers and bears—oh, my), can be added quite easily. The Cat class can also be a superclass to other classes. For example, it may be necessary to abstract the Cat class further, to provide classes for Persian cats, Siamese cats, and so on. Just as with Cat, the Dog class can be the parent for GermanShepherd and Poodle (see Figure 1.15). The power of inheritance lies in its abstraction and organization techniques.

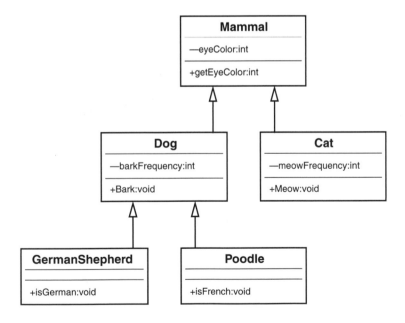

FIGURE 1.15

Mammal UML diagram.

Note that the classes GermanShepherd and Poodle both inherit from Dog—each contains only a single method. However, because they inherit from Dog, they also inherit from Mammal. Thus, the GermanShepherd and Poodle classes contain all the attributes and methods included in Dog and Mammal, as well as their own. (See Figure 1.16.)

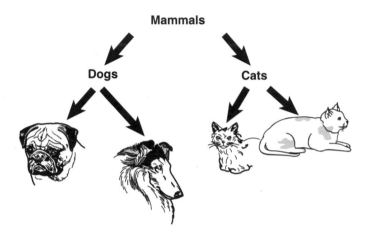

FIGURE 1.16
Mammal hierarchy.

Is-a Relationships

In the Shape example, Circle, Square, and Star all inherit directly from Shape. This relationship is often referred to as an *is-a relationship* because a circle *is a* shape. When a subclass inherits from a superclass, it can do anything that the superclass can do. Thus, Circle, Square, and Star are all extensions of Shape.

In Figure 1.17, the name on each of the objects represents the Draw method for the Circle, Star, and Square objects, respectively. The main point is that when drawing a shape, only the Draw method needs to be called, regardless of what the shape is. It is the individual object's responsibility to draw itself.

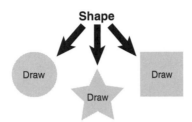

FIGURE 1.17
The shape hierarchy.

Polymorphism

Polymorphism literally means many shapes. While polymorphism is tightly coupled to inheritance, it is often cited separately as one of the most powerful advantages to object-oriented technologies. When a message is sent to an object, the object must have a method defined to respond to that message. In an inheritance hierarchy, all subclasses inherit the interfaces from their superclass. However, because each subclass is a separate entity, each may require a separate response to the same message. For example, consider a class called Shape, with a behavior called Draw. When you tell somebody to draw a shape, the first question he or she asks is What shape? He or she cannot draw a shape, it is too abstract (in fact, the Draw() method in Shape contains no implementation). You must specify a concrete shape. To do this, you provide the actual implementation in Circle. Even though Shape has a Draw method, Circle overrides this method and provides its own Draw() method. *Overriding* basically means replacing an implementation of a parent with one from a child.

For example, suppose you have an array of three shapes—Circle, Square, and Star. Even though you treat them all as Shape objects, and send a Draw message to each Shape object, the end result is different for each because Circle, Square, and Star provide the actual implementations. In short, each class is able to respond differently to the same Draw method and draw itself. This is what is meant by polymorphism.

Consider the following Shape class:

```
public abstract class Shape{

    private double area;

    public abstract double getArea();

}
```

The Shape class has an attribute called area that holds the value for the area of the shape. The method getArea() includes an identifier called abstract. When a method is defined as abstract, a subclass must provide the implementation for this method; in this case, Shape is requiring subclasses to provide a getArea() implementation. Now let's create a class called Circle that inherits from Shape (the extends keyword signifies that Circle inherits from Shape):

```java
public class Circle extends Shape{

    double radius;

    public Circle(double r) {

        radius = r;

    }

    public double getArea() {

        area = 3.14*(radius*radius);
        return (area);

    };
}
```

We introduce a new concept here called a *constructor*. The Circle class has a method with the same name, Circle. When the names are the same and no return type is provided, the method is a special method, called a constructor. Consider a constructor the entry point for the class, where the object is constructed; the constructor is a good place to perform initializations.

The Circle constructor accepts a single parameter, representing the radius, and assigns it to the radius attribute of the Circle class.

The Circle class also provides the implementation for the getArea method, originally defined as abstract in the Shape class.

We can create a similar class, called Rectangle:

```java
public class Rectangle extends Shape{

    double length;
    double width;

    public Rectangle(double l, double w){
        length = l;
        width = w;
```

```
    }

    public double getArea() {
        area = length*width;
        return (area);
    };

}
```

Now we can create a number of shapes and invoke a getArea() method because we know that all Shape classes have a getArea() method. If a subclass inherits an abstract method from a superclass, it *must* provide a concrete implementation of that method, or else it will be an abstract class itself (see Figure 1.18 for a UML diagram).

Thus, we can instantiate the Shape classes in this way:

```
Circle circle = new Circle(5);
Rectangle rectangle = new Rectangle(4,5);
```

Then, using a construct such as a stack, we can add these Shape classes to the stack:

```
stack.push(circle);
stack.push(rectangle);
```

TIP

What is a Stack?

A *stack* is a data structure that is a last-in, first-out system. It is like a coin changer, where you insert coins at the top of the cylinder and, when you need a coin, you simply take one off the top, which is the last one you inserted. Pushing an item onto the stack means that you are adding an item to the top (like inserting another coin into the changer). Popping an item off the stack means that you are taking the last item off the stack (like taking the coin off the top).

Now comes the fun part. We can empty the stack, and we do not have to care about what kind of Shape classes are in it:

```
while (  !stack.empty()) {
    Shape shape = (Shape) stack.pop();
    System.out.println ("Area = " + shape.getArea());
}
```

In reality, we are sending the same message to all the shapes:

```
shape.getArea()
```

However, the actual behavior that takes place depends on the type of shape. For example, Circle will calculate the area for a circle, and Rectangle will calculate the area of a rectangle. In effect (and here is the key concept), we are sending a message to the Shape classes and experiencing different behavior depending on what subclass of Shape is being used.

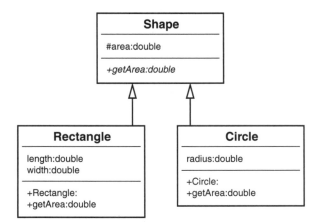

FIGURE 1.18
Shape UML diagram.

Composition

It is natural to think of objects as containing other objects. A television set contains a tuner and video display. A computer contains video cards, keyboards, and drives. Although the computer can be considered an object unto itself, the drive is also considered a valid object. In fact, you could open up the computer and remove the drive and hold it in your hand. Both the computer and the drive are considered objects. It is just that the computer contains other objects—such as drives.

In this way, objects are often built, or *composed*, from other objects: This is *composition*.

Has-a Relationships

While an inheritance relationship is considered an Is-a relationship for reasons already discussed, a composition relationship is termed a Has-a relationship. Using the example in the previous section, a television Has-a tuner and Has-a video display. A television is obviously not a tuner, so there is no inheritance relationship. In the same vein, a computer Has-a video card, Has-a keyboard, and Has-a disk drive. The topics of inheritance, composition, and how they relate to each other is covered in great detail in Chapter 8, "Frameworks and Reuse: Designing with Interfaces and Abstract Classes."

Conclusion

There is a lot to cover when discussing O-O technologies. However, you should leave this chapter with a good understanding of the following topics:

- Encapsulation. Encapsulating the data and behavior into a single object is of primary importance in O-O development. A single object contains both its data and behaviors and can hide what it wants from other objects.

- Inheritance. A class can inherit from another class and take advantage of the attributes and methods defined by the superclass.

- Polymorphism. Polymorphism means that similar objects can respond to the same message in different manners. For example, you may have a system with many shapes. However, a circle, a square, and a star are each drawn differently. Using polymorphism, you can send each of these shapes the same message (for example, Draw), and each shape is responsible for drawing itself.

- Composition. Composition means that an object is built from other objects.

This chapter covers the fundamental O-O concepts. By now you should have a good grasp of what O-O concepts are all about.

How to Think in Terms of Objects

IN THIS CHAPTER

- **Learn how to think in an object-oriented way**

- **Reinforce the difference between the implementation and the interface**

- **Give the users only what they absolutely need**

- **Think more abstractly**

In Chapter 1, "Introduction to Object-Oriented Concepts," you learned the fundamental object-oriented (O-O) concepts. The rest of the book digs more deeply into these concepts. Many factors go into a good design, whether it is an O-O design or not. The fundamental unit of O-O design is the class. The desired end result of O-O design is a robust and functional object model—a system.

As in many things in life, there is no single right or wrong way to approach a problem. There are usually many different ways to tackle the same problem. So when attempting to design an O-O solution, don't get hung up in trying to do a perfect design the first time. What you really need to do is brainstorm and let your thought process go wild. Do not try to conform to any standards or conventions when trying to solve a problem because the whole idea is to be creative. Thus, before you start to design a class, or even a system, think the problem through—have some fun! In this chapter we explore the fine art of O-O thinking.

The move from the procedural world to an O-O world is not trivial. Changing from FORTRAN to Cobol, or even to C, requires that you learn a new language; however, making the move from Cobol to C++ or Java requires that you learn a new thought process. This is where the overused phrase *O-O paradigm* rears its ugly head. When moving to an O-O language, you must go through the investment of learning O-O concepts and the corresponding thought process first. If this paradigm shift does not take place, one of two things will happen: Either the project will not truly be O-O in nature (that is, it will use C++ without using the O-O constructs), or the project will be a complete object-disoriented mess.

Three important things you can do to develop a good sense of the O-O thought process are covered in this chapter:

- Knowing the difference between the interface and implementation
- Thinking more abstractly
- Giving the user the minimal interface possible

We have already met some of these concepts in Chapter 1, and here we will now go into much more detail.

Knowing the Difference Between the Interface and the Implementation

As we saw in Chapter 1, one of the keys to O-O design is knowing the difference between the interface and the implementation. Thus, when designing a class, what the user needs to know and what the user does not need to know are of vital importance. Encapsulation is the means by which nonessential data is hidden from the user.

> **WARNING**
>
> Do not confuse the concept of the interface with terms like *graphical user interface (GUI)*. While a GUI is, as its name implies, an interface, the term interfaces, as used here, is more general in nature and is not restricted to a graphical interface.

Remember the toaster example in Chapter 1? The toaster, or any appliance for that matter, is simply plugged into the interface, which is the electrical outlet—see Figure 2.1. All appliances have access to electricity by complying with using the correct interface: the electrical outlet. The toaster doesn't need to know about the implementation, or how the electricity is produced. The electricity could be produced by a coal plant or a nuclear plant—the appliance does not care which, as long as the interface works.

As another example, consider an automobile. The interface between you and the car includes components such as steering wheels, gas pedals, brakes, and ignition switch. For most people, aesthetic issues aside, the main concern when driving a car is that the car starts, accelerates, stops, steers, and so on. The implementation, basically the stuff that you don't see, is of little concern to the average driver. In fact, most people would not even be able to identify certain components, such as the catalytic converters and gaskets. However, any driver would recognize and know how to use the steering wheel because this is a common interface. By installing a standard steering wheel in the car, manufacturers are assured that the people in their target market will be able to use the mechanism.

If, however, a manufacturer decided to install a joystick in place of the steering wheel, most drivers would balk at this, and the automobile might not be a big seller (except for some eclectic people who love bucking the trends). On the other hand, as long as the performance and aesthetics didn't change, the average driver would not notice if the manufacturer changed the engine—part of the implementation—of the automobile.

> **WARNING**
>
> It must be stressed that the interchangeable engines must be identical in every way—as far as the driver's perceptions go. Replacing a four-cylinder engine with an eight-cylinder engine would change the rules just as changing the current from AC to DC would affect the rules in the power plant example.

The engine is part of the implementation, and the steering wheel is part of the interface. A change in the implementation should have no impact on the driver, whereas a change to the interface might.

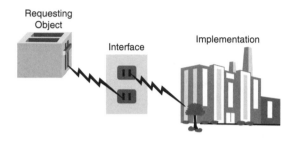

FIGURE 2.1
Power plant revisited.

TIP

What Users See

Interfaces also relate directly to classes. End users do not normally see any classes—they see the GUI or command line. However, programmers *would* see the class interfaces. Class reuse means that someone has already written a class. Thus, a programmer who uses a class must know how to use the class. This programmer will combine many classes to create a system. The programmer is the one who needs to understand the interfaces of a class. Therefore, when we talk about users in this chapter, we mean designers and developers—not end users. And when we talk about interfaces, we are talking about class interfaces, not GUIs.

To encapsulate data, classes are designed in two parts—the interface and the implementation.

The Interface

The interface is the services that are presented to an end user. In the best case, *only* the services that the end user needs are presented. Of course, which services the user needs may be a matter of opinion. If you put 10 people in a room and ask each of them to do an independent design, you might receive 10 totally different designs. There is nothing wrong with this. However, as a rule of thumb, the interface to a class should contain only what the user needs to know. In the toaster example, the user only needs to know that the toaster must be plugged into the interface—which in this case is the electrical outlet.

> **TIP**
>
> ## Identifying the User
> Perhaps the most important issue when designing a class is identifying the audience, or users, of the class.

The Implementation

The implementation details of the interface services are hidden from the user and can be changed as long as the interface remains the same. Recall that in the toaster example, although the interface is always the electric outlet, the implementation could change from a coal power plant to a nuclear power plant without affecting the toaster. There is one very important caveat to be made here: The coal or nuclear plant must also conform to the interface specification. If the coal plant produces AC power, but the nuclear plant produces DC power, then there is a problem. The bottom line is that both the user and the implementation must conform to the interface specification.

An Interface/Implementation Example

Let's create a simple (if not very functional) Oracle database reader class. We'll write some Java code that will retrieve records from the Oracle database. As we've discussed, knowing your end users is always the most important issue when doing any kind of design. You should do some analysis of the situation and conduct interviews with end users, and then list the requirements for the project. The following are some requirements we might want to use for the database reader:

- We must be able to open a connection to the database.
- We must be able to close the connection to the database.
- We must be able to position the cursor on the first record in the database.
- We must be able to position the cursor on the last record in the database.
- We must be able to find the number of records in the database.
- We must be able to determine whether there are more records in the database (that is, if we are at the end).
- We must be able to position the cursor at a specific record by supplying the key.
- We must be able to retrieve a record by supplying a key.
- We must be able to get the next record, based on the position of the cursor.

With these requirements in mind, we can make an initial attempt to design the database reader class by creating possible interfaces for these end users.

In this case, the database reader class is intended for programmers who require use of a database. Thus, the interface is essentially the application programming interface (API) that the programmer will use. These methods are, in effect, wrappers that enclose the functionality provided by the database system. Why would we do this? We will explore this question in much greater detail later in the chapter; the short answer is that we might need to customize some database functionality. For example, we might need to process the objects so that we can write them to a relational database. Writing this *middleware* is not trivial as far as design and coding go, but it is a real-life example of wrapping functionality.

Figure 2.2 shows a class diagram representing a possible interface to the DataBaseReader class.

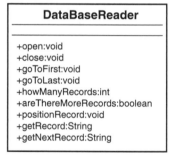

DataBaseReader

+open:void
+close:void
+goToFirst:void
+goToLast:void
+howManyRecords:int
+areThereMoreRecords:boolean
+positionRecord:void
+getRecord:String
+getNextRecord:String

FIGURE 2.2
A Unified Modeling Language class diagram for the DataBaseReader *class.*

Note that the methods in this class are all public (remember that there are plus signs next to the names of methods that are public interfaces). Also note that only the interface is represented; the implementation is not shown. Take a minute to determine if this class diagram generally satisfies the requirements outlined earlier for the project. If you find out later that the diagram does not meet all the requirements, that's okay; remember that O-O design is an iterative process, so you do not have to get it exactly right the first time.

TIP

Public Interface
Remember that if a method is public, then a programmer can access it, and thus, it is considered part of the interface.

For each of the requirements we listed, we need a corresponding method that provides the functionality we want. Now you need to ask a few questions:

- To effectively use this class, do you as a programmer need to know anything else about it?
- Do you need to know how the code actually opens the Oracle database?
- Do you need to know how the code actually positions itself over a specific record?
- Do you need to know how the code determines whether there are any more records left?

On all counts the answer is a resounding *no*! You don't need to know any of this information. All you care about is that you get the proper return values and that the operations are performed correctly. In fact, the application programmer will most likely be at least one more abstract level away from the implementation. The application will use your classes to open the database, which in turn will invoke the proper Oracle API.

Creating wrappers may seem like overkill, but there are many advantages to writing them. To illustrate, there are many middleware products on the market today. Consider the problem of mapping objects to a relational database. There are a lot of O-O databases on the market today that are perfect for O-O applications. However, there is one itty-bitty problem: Most companies have years of data in legacy, relational database systems. How can a company embrace O-O technologies and stay on the bleeding edge when its data is in a relational database?

First, you can convert all your legacy, relational data to a brand-new O-O database. Anyone who has suffered the acute (and chronic) pain of data conversions knows that this is to be avoided like the plague.

Second, you can use a middleware product to seamlessly map the objects in your application code to a relational model. This is a much better solution, at least for the short term. When using objects, O-O databases are much more efficient in object persistence than are relational databases, but in the short term, using the relational-to-object mapping is a great solution. For brand-new O-O applications that need to create new data stores, using an O-O database is a viable choice.

WARNING

Standalone Application?

Even when creating a new O-O application from scratch, it may not be easy to avoid legacy data. This is due to the fact that even a newly created O-O application is most likely not a stand-alone application and may need to exchange information stored in relational databases.

Let's return to the database example. Figure 2.2 shows the public interface to the class, and nothing else. Of course, when this class is complete, it will probably contain more methods, and it will certainly contain attributes. However, you as a programmer using this class do not need to know anything about these private methods and attributes. You don't even need to know what the code looks like within the public methods. You simply need to know how to interact with the interfaces.

What would the code for this public interface look like? Let's look at the open() method:

```
public void open(String Name){

        /* Some application-specific processing

        /* call the Oracle API to open the database */

        /* Some more application-specific processing */

};
```

In this case, you, wearing your programmer's hat, realize that the open method requires String as a parameter. Name, which represents a database file, is passed in, but it's not important to use for this example how Name is mapped to a specific database. That's all we need to know. Now comes the fun stuff—what really makes interfaces so great!

Just to annoy our users, let's change the database implementation. Last night we translated all the data from an Oracle database to a SQLAnywhere database (we endured the acute and chronic pain). It took us hours—but we did it.

Now the code looks like this:

```
public void open(String Name){

        /* Some application-specific processing

        /* call the SQLAnywhere API to open the database */

        /* Some more application-specific processing */

};
```

To our great chagrin, this morning not one user complained. Even though the implementation changed, the interface did not! As far as the user is concerned the calls are still the same. The code change for the implementation may have required quite a bit of work (and the module with the one-line code change would have to be rebuilt), but not one line of application code that uses this DataBaseReader class needed to change.

> **Tip**
>
> ### Code Recompilation
>
> In Java, because classes are loaded dynamically, no user classes would have to be recompiled. However, in statically linked languages such as C++, a link is required to bring in the new class.

By separating the user interface from the implementation, we can save a lot of headaches down the road. In Figure 2.3, the database implementations are transparent to the end users, who see only the interface.

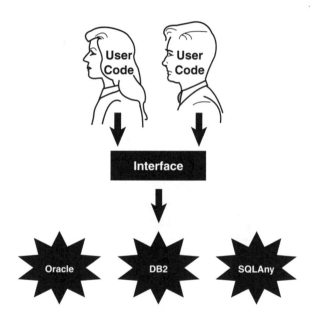

Figure 2.3
The interface.

Using Abstract Thinking when Designing Interfaces

One of the main advantages of O-O programming is that classes can be reused. In general, reusable classes tend to have interfaces that are more abstract than concrete. Concrete interfaces tend to be very specific while abstract interfaces are not. However, simply stating that a more abstract interface is more useful than a more concrete interface, while often true, is not always the case.

It is possible to write a very useful, concrete class that is not at all reusable. This happens all the time, and there is nothing wrong with it in some situations. Yet, we are now in the design business and want to take advantage of what O-O offers us. So our goal is to design abstract, highly reusable classes—and to do this we will design highly abstract user interfaces. To illustrate the difference between an abstract and a concrete interface, let's create a taxi object. It is much more useful to have an interface such as "drive me to the airport" than to have separate interfaces such as "turn right," "turn left," "start," "stop," and so on, because as illustrated in Figure 2.4, all the user wants to do is get to the airport.

When you emerge from your hotel, throw your bags into the back seat of the taxi and get in, the cabbie will turn to you and ask, "Where do you want to go?" You reply, "Please take me to the airport." (This assumes, of course, that there is only one major airport in the city. In Chicago you would have to say, "Please take me to Midway Airport" or "Please take me to O'Hare.") You might not even know how to get to the airport yourself, and even if you did, you wouldn't want to have to tell the cabbie when to turn and which direction to turn, as illustrated in Figure 2.5. How the cabbie implements the actual drive is of no concern to you, the passenger (of course the fare might become an issue at some point, if the cabbie cheats and takes you the long way to the airport).

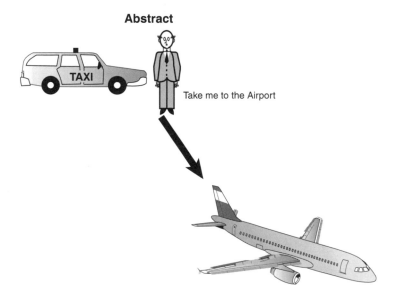

FIGURE 2.4
An abstract interface.

Not So Abstract

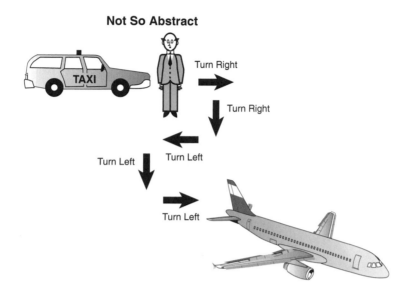

Turn Right

Turn Right

Turn Left

Turn Left

Turn Left

Turn Left

FIGURE 2.5

A not so abstract interface.

Now, where does the connection between abstract and reuse come in? Ask yourself which of these two scenarios is more reusable, the abstract or the not-so-abstract. To put it more simply, which phrase is more reusable: "Take me to the airport" or "Turn right then right then left then left then left"? Obviously, the first phrase is more reusable. You can use it in any city, whenever you get into a taxi and want to go to the airport. The second phrase will only work in a specific case. Thus, the abstract interface "Take me to the airport" is generally the way to go for a good, reusable O-O design, whose implementation would be different in Chicago, New York, or Cleveland.

Giving the User the Minimal Interface Possible

When designing a class, the rule of thumb is to always provide the user with as little knowledge of the inner workings of the class as possible. To accomplish this, follow these simple rules:

- Give the users only what they absolutely need. In effect, this means the class has as few interfaces as possible. When you start designing a class, start with a minimal interface. The design of a class is iterative, so you will soon discover that the minimal set of interfaces may not suffice. This is fine. It is better to have to add an interface because users really need it than to give the users more interfaces than they need.

For the moment, let's use a hardware example to illustrate our software example. Imagine handing a user a PC box without a monitor or a keyboard. Obviously, the PC would be of little use. You have just provided the user with the minimal set of interfaces to the PC. Of course, this minimal set is insufficient, and it immediately becomes necessary to add interfaces.

- Public interfaces are all the users will ever see. You should initially hide the entire class from the user. Then when you start using the class, you will be forced to make certain methods public—these methods thus become the public interface.

- It is vital to design classes from a user's perspective and not from an information systems viewpoint. Too often designers of classes (not to mention any other kind of software) design the class to make it fit into a specific technological model. Even if the designer takes a user's perspective, it is still probably a technician user's perspective, and the class is designed with an eye on getting it to work from a technology standpoint and not from ease of use for the user.

- Users are the ones that will actually use the software. Make sure that when you are designing a class that you go over the requirements and the design with the people who will actually use it—not just developers. The class will most likely evolve and need to be updated when a prototype of the system is built.

Determining the Users

Let's look again at the taxi example. We have already decided that the users are the ones that will actually use the system. This said, the obvious question is who are the users?

The first impulse is to say the *customers*. This is only about half right. Although the customers are certainly users, the cabbie must be able to successfully provide the service to the customers. In other words, providing an interface that would, no doubt, please the customer, like "Take me to the airport for free," is not going to go over well with the cabbie. Thus, in reality, to build a realistic and usable interface, *both* the customer and the cabbie must be considered users.

In short, any object that sends a message to the taxi object is considered a user (and yes, the users are objects, too). Figure 2.6 shows how the Cabbie provides a service.

TIP

Looking Ahead
The cabbie is most likely an object as well.

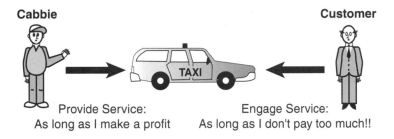

FIGURE 2.6
Providing services.

Object Behavior

Identifying the users is only a part of the exercise. After the users are identified, you must determine the behaviors of the objects. From the viewpoint of all the users, begin identifying the purpose of each object and what it must do to perform properly. Note that many of the initial choices will not survive the final cut of the public interface.

Environmental Constraints

In their book *Object-Oriented Design in Java*, Gilbert and McCarty point out that the environment often imposes limitations on what an object can do. In fact, environmental constraints are almost always a factor. Computer hardware may limit software functionality. For example, a system may not be connected to a network or a company uses a specific type of printer. In the taxi example, the cab cannot drive on a road if a bridge is out even if it provides a quicker way to the airport.

Identifying the Public Interfaces

With all the information gathered about the users, the object behaviors, and the environment, you need to determine the public interfaces for each user object. So, back with the taxi object, think about how you would use the taxi object:

- Get into the taxi.
- Tell the cabbie where you want to go.
- Pay the cabbie.
- Give the cabbie a tip.
- Get out of the taxi.

What do you need to do to use the taxi object?

- Have a place to go.
- Hail a taxi.
- Pay the cabbie money.

Initially, then, you think about how the object is used and not how it is built. You might discover that the object needs more interfaces, such as "Put luggage in the trunk" or "Enter into a mindless conversation with the cabbie." Figure 2.7 provides a class diagram that lists possible methods for the Cabbie class.

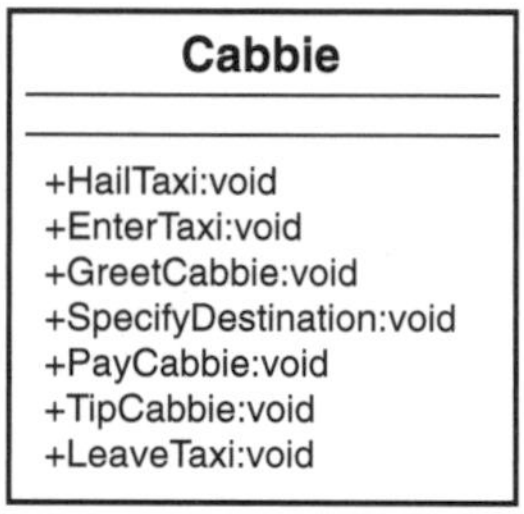

```
┌─────────────────────────────┐
│           Cabbie            │
├─────────────────────────────┤
│                             │
├─────────────────────────────┤
│ +HailTaxi:void              │
│ +EnterTaxi:void             │
│ +GreetCabbie:void           │
│ +SpecifyDestination:void    │
│ +PayCabbie:void             │
│ +TipCabbie:void             │
│ +LeaveTaxi:void             │
└─────────────────────────────┘
```

FIGURE 2.7
The methods in a cabbie class.

As is always the case, nailing down the final interface is an iterative process. For each interface, you must determine if the interface contributes to the operation of the object. If it does not, then perhaps it is not necessary. Many O-O texts recommend that each interface model only one behavior. This returns us to the question of how abstract we want to get with the design. If we have an interface called EnterTaxi(), we certainly do not want EnterTaxi() to have logic in it to pay the cabbie. If we do this, then not only is the design somewhat illogical, but there is virtually no way that a user of the class can tell what has to be done to simply pay the cabbie.

Identifying the Implementation

After the public interfaces are chosen, you need to identify the implementation. After the class is designed and all the methods required to operate the class properly are in place, the issue tends to be an either/or proposition.

Technically, anything that is not a public interface can be considered the implementation. This means that the user will never see any of the methods that are considered part of the implementation, including the method's signature as well as the actual code inside the method. The implementation is totally hidden from the user. In fact, the code within public methods is actually a part of the implementation because the user cannot see it (the user should only see the calling structure of an interface—not the code inside it).

This means that, theoretically, anything that is considered the implementation may change without affecting how the user interfaces with the class. This assumes, of course, that the implementation is providing the answers that the user expects.

Whereas the interface represents how the user sees the object, the implementation is really the nuts and bolts of the object. The implementation contains the code that represents that state of an object.

Conclusion

In this chapter we have explored three areas that can get you started on the path to thinking in an O-O way. Remember that there is no firm list of issues pertaining to the O-O thought process. Doing things in an O-O way is more of an art than a science. Try to think of your own ways to describe O-O thinking.

In Chapter 3, "Advanced Object-Oriented Concepts," we'll talk about the fact that the object has a life cycle: It is born, it lives, and it dies. While it is alive, it may transition though many different states. For example, a `DataBaseReader` object is in one state if the database is open and another state if the database is closed. How this is represented depends on the design of the class.

References

Flower, Martin: *UML Distilled*. Addison Wesley Longman, 1997.

Gilbert, Stephen, and Bill McCarty: *Object-Oriented Design in Java*. The Waite Group, 1998.

Meyers, Scott: *Effective C++*. Addison-Wesley, 1992.

Advanced Object-Oriented Concepts

IN THIS CHAPTER

- **Learn more advanced object-oriented concepts**

- **Understand how an object is created and initialized**

- **Understand how errors are handled**

- **Understand how objects are copied and compared**

Chapters 1, "An Introduction to Object-Oriented Concepts," and 2, "How to Think in Terms of Objects," cover the basics of object-oriented (O-O) concepts. Before we embark on our journey to learn some of the finer design issues relating to building an O-O system, we need to cover several more advanced O-O concepts.

Some of these concepts might not be vital to understanding an O-O design at a higher level, but they are necessary to anyone actually involved in the design and implementation of an O-O system.

Constructors

Constructors are a new concept for people doing structured programming. Constructors do not normally exist in non-O-O languages such as C and Basic. Earlier we spoke about special methods that are used to *construct* objects. In Java and C++, as well as other O-O languages, constructors are methods that share the same name as the class and have no return type. For example, a constructor for the Cabbie class would look like this:

```
public Cabbie(){
    /* code to construct the object */
}
```

The compiler will recognize that the method name is identical to the class name and consider the method a constructor.

> ### Return Value
> Note again that a constructor does not have a return value. If you provide a return value, the compiler will not treat the method as a constructor.

When Is a Constructor Called?

When a new object is created, one of the first things that happens is that the constructor is called. Check out the following code:

```
Cabbie myCabbie = new Cabbie();
```

The new keyword creates a new instance of the Cabbie class, thus allocating the required memory. Then the constructor is called, passing the arguments in the parameter list. The developer must do the appropriate initialization within the constructor.

Thus, the code new Cabbie() will instantiate a Cabbie object and call the Cabbie method, which is the constructor.

What's Inside a Constructor?

The most important function of a constructor is to initialize the memory allocated when the new keyword is encountered. In short, code included inside a constructor should set the newly created object to its initial, stable state.

For example, if you have a counter object with an attribute called count, you need to set count to zero in the constructor:

```
count = 0;
```

> ## Initializing Attributes
> Initializing attributes is a common function performed within a constructor.

The Default Constructor

If you write a class and do not include a constructor, the class will still compile and you can still use it. If the class provides no explicit constructor, such as in C++ and Java, a default constructor will be provided.

The default constructor calls only the constructor of the superclass. For example, if a constructor is not provided for the Cabbie class, the following default constructor is inserted:

```
public Cabbie(){
    super();
}
```

Perhaps the default constructor may be sufficient in some cases; however, in most cases some sort of memory initialization should be performed. Regardless of the situation, it is good programming practice to always include at least one constructor in a class. In any case, if there are attributes in the class, they should be initialized in a constructor.

> ## Providing a Constructor
> The rule of thumb is that you should *always* provide a constructor, even if you do not plan on doing anything inside it. You can provide a constructor with nothing in it and then add to it later. While there is technically nothing wrong with using the default constructor provided by the compiler, it is always nice to know exactly what your code looks like.

Using Multiple Constructors

In many cases, an object can be constructed in more than one way. To accommodate this situation you need to provide more than one constructor. For example, let's consider the `Count` class presented below.

```
public class Count {

    int count;

    public Count(){
        count = 0;
    }
}
```

On the one hand we simply want to initialize the attribute `count` to count to zero: We can easily accomplish this by having a constructor initialize `count` to zero as follows:

```
public Count(){
    count = 0;
}
```

On the other hand, we might want to pass an initialization parameter that allows `count` to be set to various numbers:

```
public Count (int number){
    count = number;
}
```

This is called *overloading a method* (overloading pertains to all methods, not just constructors). Most O-O languages provide functionality for overloading a method.

Overloading Methods

Overloading allows a programmer to use the same method name over and over, as long as the signature of the method is different each time. The signature consists of the method name and a parameter list (see Figure 3.1).

Thus, the following methods *all* have different signatures:

```
public void getCab();


// different parameter list
public void getCab (String cabbieName);

// different parameter list
public void getCab (int numberOfPassengers);
```

Signature

public String getRecord(int key)

$$\text{Signature} = \underset{\text{method name + parameter list}}{\text{getRecord} \qquad \text{(int key)}}$$

FIGURE 3.1

The components of a signature.

By using different signatures, you can construct objects differently depending on the constructor used.

Using UML to Model Classes

Let's return to the database reader example we used earlier in Chapter 2. Consider that we have two ways we can construct a database reader:

- Pass the name of the database and position the cursor at the beginning of the database.
- Pass the name of the database and the position within the database where we want the cursor to position itself.

Figure 3.2 shows a class diagram for the DataBaseReader class. Note that the diagram lists two constructors for the class. While the diagram shows the two constructors, without the parameter list there is no way to know which constructor is which. To distinguish the constructors, you can look at the corresponding code listed below.

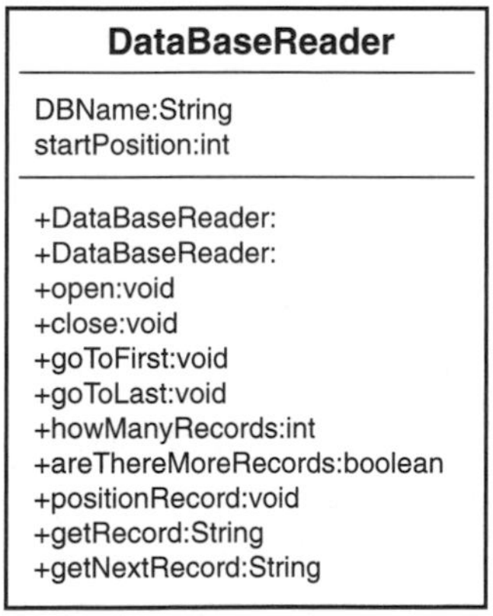

DataBaseReader
DBName:String startPosition:int
+DataBaseReader: +DataBaseReader: +open:void +close:void +goToFirst:void +goToLast:void +howManyRecords:int +areThereMoreRecords:boolean +positionRecord:void +getRecord:String +getNextRecord:String

FIGURE 3.2

The DataBaseReader class diagram.

No Return Type

Notice that in this class diagram the constructors do not have a return type. All other methods besides constructors must have return types.

Here is a code segment of the class that shows its constructors and the attributes that the constructors initialize (see Figure 3.3):

```
public class DataBaseReader {

    String DBName;
    int startPosition;

    // initialize just the name
    public DataBaseReader (String name){
    DBName = name;
};

    // initialize the name and the position
    public DataBaseReader (String name, int pos){
        DBName = name;
        startPosition = pos;
    };

    .. // rest of class
}
```

How the Superclass Is Constructed

When using inheritance, you must know how the parent class is constructed. Remember that when you use inheritance, you are inheriting everything about the parent. Thus, you must become intimately aware of all the parent's data and behavior. The inheritance of an attribute is fairly obvious. However, how a constructor is inherited is not as obvious. After the new keyword is encountered and the object is allocated, the following steps occur (see Figure 3.4):

1. The first thing that happens inside the constructor is that the constructor of the class's superclass is called.

2. Then each class attribute of the object is initialized. These are the attributes that are part of the class definition (instance variables), not the attributes inside the constructor or any other method (local variables). In the DataBaseReader code presented earlier, the integer startposition is an instance variable of the class.

3. Then the rest of the code in the constructor executes.

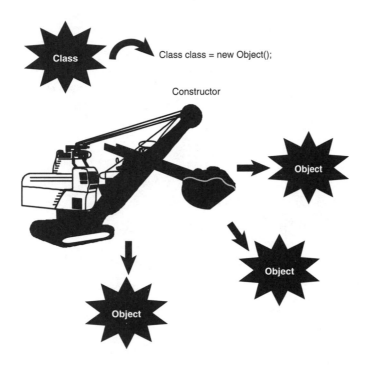

FIGURE 3.3
Creating a new object.

Constructing an Object

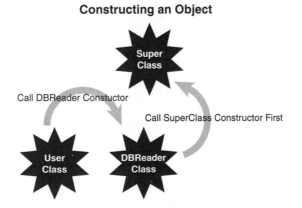

FIGURE 3.4
Constructing an object.

The Design of Constructors

When designing a class, it is good practice to initialize all the attributes. In some languages, the compiler might attempt to do this initialization. As always, don't count on the compiler to initialize attributes! In Java, you cannot use an attribute until it is initialized. If the attribute is first set in the code, make sure that you initialize the attribute to some valid condition—for example, set an integer to zero.

Constructors are used to ensure that the application is in a stable state. For example, initializing an attribute to zero, when it is intended for use as a denominator in a division operation, may lead to an unstable application. You must take into consideration the fact that a division by zero is an illegal operation.

During the design, it is good practice to identify a stable state for all attributes and then initialize them to this stable state in the constructor.

Error Handling

It is rare for a class to be written perfectly the first time. In most, if not all, situations, things *will* go wrong. Any designer who does not plan for problems is courting danger.

Assuming that your code has the ability to detect and trap an error condition, you can handle the error in several different ways: In a training class based on their book *Java Primer Plus*, page 223, by Tyma, Torok and Downing, the authors state that there are three basic solutions to handling problems that are detected in a program: fix it, ignore the problem by squelching it, and exit the runtime in some graceful manner. Gilbert and McCarty, in their book *Object-Oriented Design in Java*, on page 139, basically state the same thing but add the choice of throwing an exception:

- Ignore the problem—not a good idea!
- Check for potential problems and abort the program when you find a problem.
- Check for potential problems, catch the mistake, and attempt to fix the problem.
- Throw an exception. (This is the preferred way to handle the situation.)

These strategies are discussed in the following sections.

Ignoring the Problem

Simply ignoring a potential problem is a recipe for disaster. And if you are going to ignore the problem, why bother detecting it in the first place? The bottom line is that you should not ignore the problem. The primary directive for all applications is that the application should never crash. If you do not handle your errors, the application will eventually terminate ungracefully or continue in a mode that can be considered an unstable state. In the latter case, you might not even know it for some period of time.

Checking for Problems and Aborting the Application

If you choose to check for potential problems and abort the application when a problem is detected, whenever a problem is detected, the application displays a message saying that you have a problem. Then the code gracefully exits and the user is left staring at the computer screen, shaking his or her head and wondering what bus just happened. While this is a far superior option to ignoring the problem, it is by no means optimal. However, this does allow the system to clean up things and put itself in a more stable state, such as closing files.

Checking for Problems and Attempting to Recover

Checking for potential problems, catching the mistake, and attempting to recover is a tremendously better solution than simply checking for problems and aborting. In this case, the problem is detected by the code, and the application attempts to fix itself. This works well in certain situations. For example, consider the following code:

```
if (a == 0)
    a=1;

c = b/a;
```

It is obvious that if the `if` statement is not included in the code, and a zero makes its way to the divide statement, you will get a system exception because you cannot divide by zero. By catching the exception and setting a to 1, at least the system will not crash. However, setting a to 1 may not be a proper solution. You may need to prompt the user for the proper input value.

Although this means of error checking is preferable to the previous solutions, it still has a few potentially limiting problems. It is not always easy to determine where a problem first appears. And it might take a while for the problem to be detected. In any event, it is beyond the scope of this book to explain error handling in great detail. However, it is important to design error handling into the class right from the start.

Throwing an Exception

Most O-O languages provide a feature called *exceptions*. In the most basic sense, exceptions are errors that occur within a system. Exceptions provide a way to detect problems and then handle them. In Java and C++, exceptions are handled by the keywords `catch` and `throw`. This may sound like a baseball game, but the key here is that a specific block of code is written to handle a specific exception. This solves the problem of trying to figure out where the problem started and unwinding the code to the proper point.

Here is how the code for a try/catch block looks:

```
try {

    // possible nasty code

} catch(Exception e) {

    // code to handle the exception
}
```

If an exception is thrown within the try block, the catch block will handle it. When an exception is thrown while the block is executing, the following occurs:

1. The execution of the block is terminated.
2. The catch clauses are checked to determine whether an appropriate catch block for the offending exception was included (there may be more than one catch clause).
3. If none of the catch clauses handles the offending exception, then it is passed to the next higher-level try block (if the exception is not caught in the code, then the system ultimately catches it and the results are unpredictable).
4. If a catch clause is matched (the first match encountered), the statements in the catch clause are executed.
5. Then execution resumes with the statement following the try block.

Again, it is beyond the scope of this book to explain exception handling in great detail. Suffice it to say that exceptions are an important advantage for O-O programming languages. Here is an example of how an exception is caught in Java:

```
try {

    // possible nasty code
    count = 0;
    count = 5/count;

} catch(ArithmeticException e) {

    // code to handle the exception
    System.out.println(e.getMessage());
    count = 1;

}
System.out.println("The exception is handled.");
```

> ## Exception Granularity
> You can catch exceptions at various levels of granularity. You can catch all exceptions or just check for specific exceptions, such as arithmetic exceptions. If your code does not catch an exception, the Java runtime will—and it won't be happy about it!

In this example, the division by zero (because count is equal to 0) within the try block will cause an arithmetic exception. If the exception was generated (thrown) outside a try block, then the program would most likely have been terminated. However, because the exception was thrown within a try block, the catch block is checked to see if the specific exception (in this case, an arithmetic exception) was planned for. Because the catch block contains a check for the arithmetic exception, the code within the catch block is executed, thus setting count to 1. After the catch block executes, the try/catch block is exited and the message, The exception is handled. appears on the Java console (see Figure 3.5).

FIGURE 3.5

Catching an exception.

If you had not put ArithmeticException in the catch block, then the program would likely have crashed. You can catch all exceptions by using the following code:

```
try {

    // possible nasty code

} catch(Exception e) {

    // code to handle the exception
}
```

The Exception parameter in the catch block is used to catch any exception that might be generated within a try block.

> ## Bulletproof Code
> It's a good idea to use a combination of the methods described here to make your program as bulletproof to your user as possible.

The Concept of Scope

Multiple objects can be instantiated from a single class. Each of these objects has its own identity and state. This is an important point. Each object is constructed separately and is allocated its own memory. However, some attributes and methods may be shared by all the objects instantiated from the same class, thus sharing the memory allocated for these class attributes and methods.

> ## A Shared Method
> A constructor is a good example of a method that is shared by all instances of a class.

Although a method generally represents the behavior of an object, the state of the object is normally represented by attributes. There are three types of attributes:

- Local attributes
- Object attributes
- Class attributes

Local Attributes

Local attributes are local to a specific method. Consider the following code:

```
public class Number {

    public method1() {
        int count;

    }

    public method2() {

    }

}
```

The method method1 contains a local variable called count. This integer is accessible only inside method1. The method method2 has no idea that the integer count exists.

At this point we can touch on a very important concept: *scope*. Attributes exist within a particular scope. In this case, the integer count exists within the scope of method1. In Java and C++, scope is delineated by curly braces ({}). In the Number class, there are several possible scopes—just start matching the curly braces.

The class itself has its own scope. Each instance of the class (that is, each object) has its own scope. Both method1 and method2 have their own scopes as well. Because count lives within method1's curly braces, when method1 is invoked, a copy of count is created. When method1 terminates, the copy of count is deleted.

For some more fun, look at this code:

```
public class Number {

    public method1() {
        int count;

    }

    public method2() {
        int count;
    }

}
```

How can this be? There are two copies of an integer count in this class. Remember that method1 and method2 each has its own scope. Thus, the compiler can tell which copy of count to access simply by recognizing which method it is in. You can think of it in these terms:

```
method1->count;
```

```
method2->count;
```

As far as the compiler is concerned, the two attributes are easily differentiated, even though they have the same name. It is almost like two people having the same last name, but based on the context of their first names, you know that they are two separate individuals.

Object Attributes

There are many design situations in which an attribute must be shared by several methods within the same object. In Figure 3.6, for example, three objects have been constructed from a single class. Consider the following code:

```
public class Number {

    int count;

    public method1() {
        count = 1;
    }

    public method2() {
        count = 2;
    }

}
```

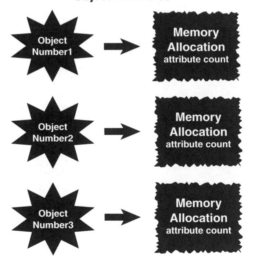

FIGURE 3.6
Object attributes.

In this case, the attribute count is declared outside the scope of both method1 and method2. However, it is within the scope of the class. Thus, count is available to both method1 and method2 (basically all methods in the class have access to this attribute). Notice that the code for both methods is setting count to a specific value. There is only one copy of count for the entire object, so both assignments operate on the same copy in memory. However, this copy of count is *not* shared between different objects.

To illustrate, let's create three copies of the `Number` class:

```
Number Number1 = new Number ();
Number Number2 = new Number ();
Number Number3 = new Number ();
```

Each of these objects—`Number1`, `Number2`, and `Number3`—is constructed separately and is allocated its own resources. There are actually three separate instances of the integer a. When `Number1` changes its attribute `count`, this in no way affects the copy of `count` in object `Number2` or object `Number3`. In this case, integer `count` is an *object attribute*.

You can play some interesting games with scope. Take a look at the following code:

```
public class Number {

    int count;

    public method1() {
        int count;
    }

    public method2() {
        int count;
    }

}
```

In this case there are actually three copies of `count`. The object has one copy, and `method1()` and `method2()` each have a copy of their own.

To access the object variable from within one of the methods, say `method1()`, you can use the following code:

```
public method1() {
        int count;

        this.count = 1;
    }
```

Notice that there is some code that looks a bit weird:

```
this.count = 1;
```

The selection of the word `this` as a keyword is, perhaps unfortunate. However, we must live with it. The use of the `this` keyword directs the compiler to access the object variable `count`, and not the local variables within the method bodies.

> ## The this Keyword
> In Java, the keyword this is a reference to the current object.

Class Attributes

As mentioned earlier, it is possible for two or more objects to share attributes. In Java and C++ you do this by making the attribute *static*:

```
public class Count {

    static int count;

    public method1() {
    }

}
```

By declaring count as static, this attribute is allocated a single piece of memory for the class. Thus, all objects of the class use the same memory location for a. Essentially, each class has a single copy, which is shared by all objects of that class (see Figure 3.7).

Class Attribute

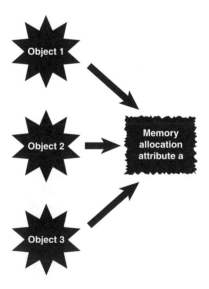

FIGURE 3.7
Class attributes.

There are many valid uses for class attributes; however, you must be aware of potential synchronization problems. Let's instantiate two `Count` objects:

```
Count Count1 = new Count();
Count Count2 = new Count();
```

For the sake of argument, let's say that the object `Count1` is going merrily about its way and is using `count` as a means to keep track of the pixels on a computer screen. This is not a problem until the object `Count2` decides to use attribute `count` to count sheep. The instant that `Count2` records its first sheep, the data that `Count1` was saving is lost.

Operator Overloading

Some O-O languages allow you to overload an operator. C++ is an example of one such language. Operator overloading allows you to change the meaning of an operator. For example, most people, when they see a plus sign, assume that it represents addition. If you see this equation

```
X = 5 + 6;
```

you expect that `X` would contain the value `11`. And in this case, you would be correct.

However, there are times when a plus sign could represent something else. For example, in the following code:

```
String firstName = "Joe", lastName = "Smith";

String Name = firstName + " " + lastName;
```

You would expect that `Name` would contain `Joe Smith`. The plus sign here has been overloaded to perform string concatenation.

String Concatenation
String concatenation is when two strings are combined to create a single string.

In the context of strings, the plus sign does not mean addition of integers or floats, but concatenation of strings.

What about matrix addition? You could have code like this:

```
Matrix A, B, C;

C = A + B;
```

Thus, the plus sign now performs matrix addition, not addition of integers or floats.

Overloading is a powerful mechanism. However, it can be downright confusing for people who read and maintain code. In fact, developers can confuse themselves.

Java does not allow the option of overloading operators. The language itself does overload the plus sign for string concatenation, but that is it. The designers of Java must have decided that operator overloading was more of a problem than it was worth. If you must use operator overloading, take care not to confuse the people who will use the class.

Multiple Inheritance

We cover inheritance in much more detail in Chapter 7, "Mastering Inheritance and Composition"; however, this is a good place to begin discussing multiple inheritance, which is one of the more powerful and challenging aspects of class design.

As the name implies, *multiple inheritance* allows a class to inherit from more than one class. In practice this seems like a great idea. Objects are supposed to model the real world, are they not? And there are many real-world examples of multiple inheritance. Parents are a good example of multiple inheritance. Each child has two parents—that's just the way it is. So it makes sense that you can design classes by using multiple inheritance. And in some O-O languages, such as C++, you can.

However, this situation falls into a category similar to operator overloading. Multiple inheritance is a very powerful technique, and in fact, some problems are quite difficult to do without it. Multiple inheritance can even solve some problems quite elegantly. However, multiple inheritance can significantly increase the complexity of a system.

As with operator overloading, the designers of Java decided that the increased complexity of allowing multiple inheritance far outweighed its advantages, so they eliminated it from the language. In some ways, the Java language construct of interfaces compensates for this; however, the bottom line is that Java does not allow conventional multiple inheritance.

Behavioral and Implementation Inheritance

Java interfaces are a mechanism for behavioral inheritance, whereas abstract classes are used for implementation inheritance. The bottom line is that Java interfaces provide interfaces, but no implementation, whereas abstract classes may provide both interfaces and implementation. This topic is covered in great detail in Chapter 8, "Frameworks and Reuse: Designing with Interfaces and Abstract Classes."

Object Operations

Some of the most basic operations in programming become more complicated when you're dealing with complex data structures and objects. For example, when you want to copy primitive data types, the process is quite straightforward. However, copying objects is not quite as simple. In his book *Effective C++,* on page 34, Scott Meyers devotes an entire section to copying and assigning objects.

Classes and References

The problem with complex data structures and objects is that they may contain references. Simply making a copy of the pointer does not copy the data structures or object that it references.

The problems arise when comparisons and copies are performed on objects. Specifically, the question boils down to whether or not you follow the pointers or not. For example, there should be a way to copy an object. Again, this is not as simple as it may seem. Since objects may contain references, these reference trees must be followed to do a valid copy (if you truly want to do a deep copy).

Deep Versus Shallow Copies

A *deep copy* is when all the references are followed and new copies are created for all referenced objects. There may be many levels involved in a deep copy. For objects with references to many objects, which in turn may have references to even more objects, the copy itself can create significant overhead. A *shallow copy* would simply copy the reference and not follow the levels. Gilbert and McCarty have a good discussion about what shallow and deep hierarchies are on page 265 of *Object-Oriented Design in Java* in a section called "Prefer a Tree to a Forest."

To illustrate, in Figure 3.8, if you just do a simple copy of the object (called a *bitwise copy*), then any object that the primary object references will not be copied—only the references will be copied. Thus, both objects (the original and the copy) will point to the same objects. To perform a complete copy, in which all reference objects are copied, you have to write the code to create all the subobjects.

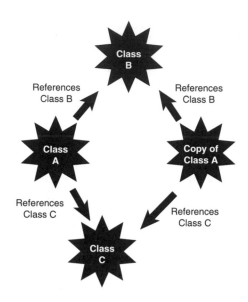

FIGURE 3.8
Following object references.

This problem also manifests itself when comparing objects. As in the copy function, this is not as simple as it may seem. Because objects contain references, these reference trees must be followed to do a valid comparison of objects. In most cases, languages provides a default mechanism to compare objects. As is usually the case, do not count on the default mechanism. When designing a class, you should consider providing a comparison function in your class that you know will behave as you want it to.

Conclusion

This chapter covers a number of advanced O-O concepts that, although perhaps not vital to a general understanding of O-O concepts, are quite necessary in the higher-level O-O tasks such as designing a class. In Chapter 4, "The Anatomy of a Class," we start looking specifically at how to design and build a class.

References

Gilbert, Stephen, and Bill McCarty: *Object-Oriented Design in Java*. The Waite Group, 1998.

Tyma, Paul, Gabriel Torok and Troy Downing: *Java Primer Plus*. The Waite Group, 1996.

Meyers, Scott: *Effective C++*. Addison-Wesley, 1992.

The Anatomy of a Class

IN THIS CHAPTER

- **Recognize what a Java class looks like**
- **Understand how to represent the interface and implementation of a class**
- **Understand how to create methods to hide and manipulate data**

We have already discussed in great detail object-oriented (O-O) concepts and the difference between the interface and the implementation. No matter how well you think out the problem of what should be an interface and what should be part of the implementation, the bottom line always comes down to how useful the class is and how it interacts with other classes. A class should never be designed in a vacuum, for as they say, no class is an island. When objects are instantiated, they almost always interact with other objects. An object may also be used within another object or may be inherited. The following section is a bit of a dissection of a class, and the rest of the chapter offers some guidelines that you should consider when designing classes.

In this chapter we'll examine a simple class and then take it apart piece by piece. See Figure 4.1 for the class that will be dissected. We will continue using the cabbie example that was presented in Chapter 2, "How to Think in Terms of Objects."

In this chapter we will discuss the following parts of a class:

- The Class Name—How the class name is identified.
- Comments—How to create comments to document your code.
- Attributes—How to define attribute for use in the class.
- Constructors—Constructors are special methods used to properly initialize a class.
- Accessors—Accessors are methods that are used to control access to private attributes.
- Public Interface Methods—How to define public interface methods.
- Private Implementation Methods—How to define private implementation methods.

TIP

Only a Template

Note that this class is meant for illustration purposes only. Some of the methods are not fleshed out (meaning that there is no implementation) and simply present the interface.

The Name of the Class

Plain and simple, the name of the class, in our example, `Cabbie`, is the name located after the keyword `class`:

```
public class Cabbie {

}
```

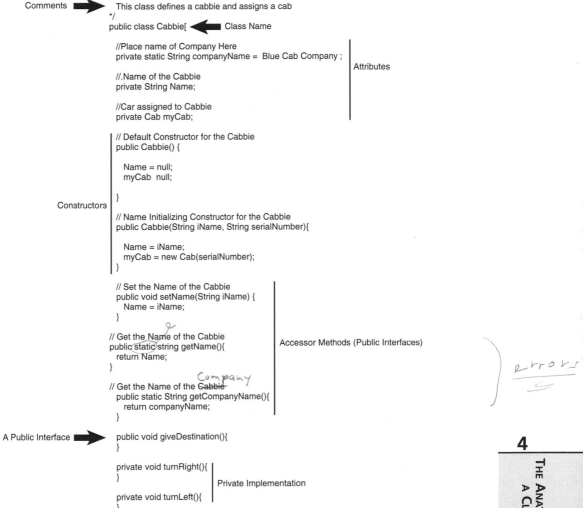

FIGURE 4.1

Our sample class.

> **TIP**
>
> ## Using Java Syntax
>
> Remember that the convention for this book is to use Java syntax. The syntax is somewhat different in C++ and totally different in other O-O languages such as Smalltalk.

The class `Cabbie` name is used whenever this class is instantiated.

Comments

Regardless of the syntax of the comments used, they are vital to understanding the function of a class. In Java and C++, there are two kinds of comments.

> **TIP**
>
> ## The Extra Java Comment Style
>
> In Java there are actually three types of comments. The third (/** */) relates to a form of documentation that Java provides. We will not cover this type of comment in this book.

The first comment is the old C-style comment, which uses /* (slash-asterisk) to open the comment andT */ (asterisk-slash) to close the comment. This type of comment can span more than one line, and it's important not to forget to use the pair of open and close comment symbols for each comment. If you miss the closing comment (*/), then some of your code may be tagged as a comment and overlooked by the compiler. Here is an example of this type of comment used with the `Cabbie` class:

```
/*

  This class defines a cabbie and assigns a cab

*/
```

The second type of comment is the // (slash-slash), which renders everything after it, to the end of the line, a comment. This type of comment spans only one line, so you don't need to remember to use a close comment symbol, but you do need to remember to confine the comment to just one line and not include any live code after the comment. Here is an example of this type of comment used with the `Cabbie` class:

```
// Name of the cabbie
```

Attributes

Attributes represent the state of the object because they store the information about the object. For our example, the `Cabbie` class has attributes that store the name of the company, the name of the cabbie, and the cab assigned to the cabbie. For example, the first attribute stores the name of the company:

```
private static String companyName = "Blue Cab Company";
```

Note here the two keywords `private` and `static`. The keyword `private` signifies that a method or variable can be accessed only within the declaring.

TIP

Hiding as Much Data as Possible

Note that all the attributes in this example are private. This is in keeping with the design principle of keeping the design as minimal as possible. The only way to access these attributes is through the method interfaces provided (which we will explore later in this chapter).

The `static` keyword signifies that there will be only one copy of this attribute for all the objects instantiated by this class. Basically, this is a class attribute. (See Chapter 3, "Advanced Object-Oriented Concepts," for more discussion on class attributes.) Thus, even if 500 objects are instantiated from the `Cabbie` class, there will be only one copy of the `companyName` attribute (see Figure 4.2).

The second attribute, `Name`, is a string that holds the name of the cabbie:

```
private String Name;
```

This attribute is also private so that other objects cannot access it directly. They must use the interface methods.

The `myCab` attribute is a reference to another object. The class, called `Cab`, holds information about the cab, such as its serial number and maintenance records:

```
private Cab myCab;
```

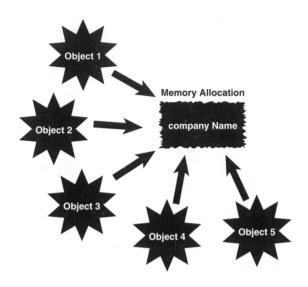

FIGURE 4.2
Object memory allocation.

TIP

Passing a Reference

It is likely that the Cab object was created by another object. Thus, the object reference would be passed to the Cabbie object. However, for the sake of this example, the Cab is created within the Cabbie object. Likewise, for the purposes of this example, we are not really interested in the internals of the Cab object.

Note that at this point, only a reference to a Cab object is created; there is no memory allocated by this definition.

Constructors

This Cabbie class contains two constructors. We know they are constructors because they have the same name as the class: Cabbie. The first constructor is the default constructor:

```
public void Cabbie() {

    Name = null;
    myCab = null;

}
```

Technically, this is not a default constructor. A default constructor would be provided by the compiler if you did not specify a constructor for this class. The reason it is called a default constructor here is because it is a constructor with no arguments.

In this constructor the attributes `Name` and `myCab` are set to `null`:

```
Name = null;
myCab = null;
```

TIP

The Nothingness of Null

In many programming languages, the value `null` represents a value of nothing. This may seem like an esoteric concept, but setting an attribute to nothing is a useful programming technique. Checking a variable for `null` can identify whether a value has been properly initialized. For example, you might want to declare an attribute that requires user input before the user is actually given the opportunity to enter the data. By setting the attribute to `null` (which is a valid condition), you can check whether an attribute has been properly set or not.

It is always a good idea to initialize attributes in the constructors. A good programming practice is to then test the value of an attribute to see if it is `null`. This can save you a lot of headaches later if the attribute or object was not set properly. For example, if your code expects that the reference to the `Cab` object, `myCab`, references an actual `Cab` object, an exception may be generated if you treat an uninitialized reference as if it were properly initialized.

The second constructor provides a way for the user of the class to initialize the `Name` and `myCab` attributes:

```
public void Cabbie(String iName, String serialNumber) {

    Name = iName;
    myCab = new Cab(serialNumber);

}
```

In this case the user would provide two strings in the parameter list of the constructor to properly initialize attributes. Notice that the `Cab` object is actually instantiated in this constructor:

```
myCab = new Cab(serialNumber);
```

4

At this point the storage for a `Cab` object is allocated. Figure 4.3 illustrates how a new instance of a `Cab` object is referenced by the attribute `myCab`. Using two constructors in this example demonstrates a common use of method overloading. Notice that the constructors are all defined as `public`. This makes sense because in this case the constructors are obvious members of the class interface.

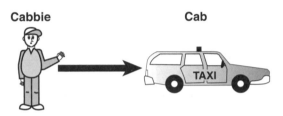

The Cabbie Object References
an Actual Cab Object

Cabbie   **Cab**

myCab = new Cab (serialNumber);

FIGURE 4.3
The Cabbie *object referencing an actual cab object.*

Accessors

In almost all examples in this book, the attributes are defined as `private` so that one class cannot access another class's attributes. So how do other classes get information about an attribute? Isn't it necessary to inspect and sometimes change another class's attribute? The answer to the last question is yes, of course. There are times when a class needs to access another's attributes; however, it does not need to do it directly.

A class should be very protective about its attributes. You do not want other classes to have the ability to change the attributes without the owner class having control. There are several reasons for this; the most important reasons really boil down to data integrity and efficient debugging.

Assume that there is a bug in the `Cab` class. You have tracked the problem to the `Name` attribute. Somehow it is getting overwritten, and garbage is turning up in some name queries. If `Name` were public and any class could change it, you would have to go searching through all possible code, trying to find places that reference and change `Name`. However, if you had let only a `Cabbie` object change `Name`, then you only have to look in the `Cabbie` class. This access is provided by a type of method called an *accessor*. Sometimes accessors are referred to as getters and setters, and sometimes they're simply called `get()` and `set()`. By convention, in this book we name the methods with the `set` and `get` prefixes, as in the following:

```
// Set the Name of the Cabbie
public void setName(String iName) {
    Name = iName;
}

// Get the Name of the Cabbie
public String getName() {
    return Name;
}
```

In this snippet, the `Supervisor` object must ask the `Cabbie` object to return its name (see Figure 4.4). The important point here is that the `Supervisor` object can't simply retrieve the information on its own, it must ask the `Cabbie` object for the information.

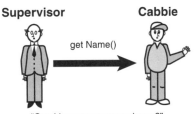

FIGURE 4.4

Asking for information.

Notice that the `getCompanyName` method is declared as `static`, as a class method; class methods are described in more detail in Chapter 3. Remember that the attribute `companyName` is also declared as static. A method, like an attribute, can be declared `static` to indicate that there is only one copy of the method for the entire class.

4

WARNING

Actually, there is not a physical copy of each nonstatic method for each object. Each object would point to the same physical code. However, from a conceptual level you can think of objects as being wholly independent and having their own attributes and methods.

The following code fragment illustrates how to define a static method and Figure 4.5 shows how more than one object points to the same code.

```
// Get the Name of the Cabbie
public static String getCompanyName() {
    return companyName;
}
```

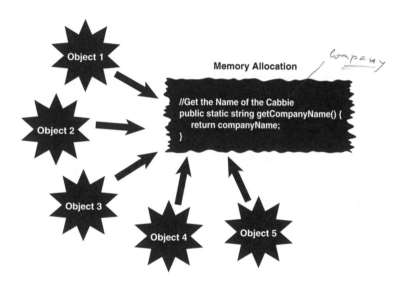

FIGURE 4.5
Method memory allocation.

Public Interface Methods

Both the constructors and the accessor methods are declared as public and are part of the public interface. They are singled out because of their specific importance to the construction of the class. However, much of the *real* work is provided in other methods. As mentioned in Chapter 2, the public interface methods tend to be very abstract, and the implementation tends to be more concrete. For this class, we provide a method called `giveDestination` that is the public interface for the user to describe where he or she wants to go:

```
public void giveDestination (){

}
```

What is inside of this method is not important at this time. The main point here is that this is a public method, and it is part of the public interface to the class.

Private Implementation Methods

Although all the methods discussed so far in this chapter are defined as `public`, not all the methods in a class are part of the public interface. Some methods in a class are meant to be hidden from other classes. These methods are declared as `private`:

```
private void turnRight(){
}

 private void turnLeft() {
}

}
```

These private methods are simply meant to be part of the implementation, and not the public interface. You might ask who invokes these methods, if no other class can. The answer is simple and you may have already surmised that these methods are called internally from the class itself. For example, these methods could be called from within the method `giveDirections`:

```
public void giveDestination (){

    .. some code

    turnRight();
    turnLeft();

    .. some more code

}
```

The point here is that private methods are strictly part of the implementation and are not accessible by other classes.

Conclusion

In this chapter we have gotten inside a class and described the fundamental concepts necessary for understanding how a class is built. Whereas this chapter takes a practical approach to discussing classes, Chapter 5, "Class Design Guidelines," covers the class from a general design perspective.

References

Flower, Martin: *UML Distilled*. Addison Wesley Longman, 1997.

Gilbert, Stephen, and Bill McCarty: *Object-Oriented Design in Java*. The Waite Group, 1998.

Tyma, Paul, Gabriel Torok and Troy Downing: *Java Primer Plus*. The Waite Group, 1996.

Class Design Guidelines

IN THIS CHAPTER

- Learn to develop a set of class design guidelines

- Understand that classes must work with other classes

- Explore the iterative nature of the class design process

One of the primary goals of object-oriented (O-O) programming is to model the ways people think, and designing classes is the way that these models are created. Rather than use a structured, or top-down, approach where data and behavior are separate, the O-O approach encapsulates the data and behavior into objects that interact with each other. Do not think of a problem as a sequence of events in various programs as you do in a structured programming. Think of how your objects model real-world objects and how they interact with other real-world objects.

These interactions occur in a way similar to interactions between real-world objects, such as people. Thus, when creating classes, you should design them in a way that represents the true behavior of the object. Let's use the cabbie example from previous chapters. The Cab class and the Cabbie class model a real-world entity. The Cab and the Cabbie objects encapsulate their data and behavior, and they interact through each other's public interfaces.

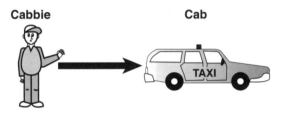

FIGURE 5.1
A cabbie and a cab are real-world objects.

When moving to O-O programming for the first time, many people tend to still think in a structured way. One of the primary mistakes is to create a class that has behavior but no class data. In effect, they are creating a set of functions or subroutines. This is not what you want to do because it violates the concept of encapsulation.

As we have already discussed, O-O programming supports the idea of making classes that are complete packages, encapsulating data and behavior of a single entity. So a class should represent a logical component, such as a taxi cab.

This chapter presents several suggestions for designing solid classes. Obviously no list such as this can be considered complete. You will undoubtedly add many guidelines to your personal list.

One of the better books pertaining to class design guidelines and suggestions is *Effective C* by Scott Meyers. In this book the subtitle is *50 Specific Ways to Improve Your Programs and Designs*. It offers important information about program design in a very concise manner.

Identifying the Public Interfaces

It should be clear by now that perhaps the most important issue when designing a class is to keep the public interface to a minimum. The entire purpose of building a class is to provide something useful and concise. Gilbert and McCarty, in their book *Object-Oriented Design in Java*, on page 109, state that *the interface of a well-designed object describes the services that the client wants accomplished*. If a class does not provide a useful service to a user, then it should not have been built in the first place.

Providing the minimum public interface makes the class as concise as possible. The goal is to provide the user with the exact interface to do the job right. If the public interface is incomplete (that is, there is missing behavior), then the user will not be able to do the complete job. If the public interface is not properly restricted (that is, the user has access to behavior that is unnecessary or even dangerous), then problems can result in the need for debugging and even trouble with system integrity. Creating a class is a business proposition, and as with all steps in the design process, it is very important that the users are involved with the design right from the start and through the testing phase. In this way, the utility of the class, as well as the proper interfaces, will be assured.

Extending the Interface

Even if the public interface of a class is insufficient for a certain application, object technology easily allows the ability to extend and adapt this interface by means of inheritance. In short, if designed with inheritance in mind, a new class can inherit from an existing class and create a new class with an extended interface.

To illustrate, consider the cabbie example once again. If other objects in the system need to get the name of a cabbie, then the `Cabbie` class must provide a public interface to return its name; this is the `getName()` method. Thus, if a `Supervisor` object needs a name from a `Cabbie` object, then it must invoke the `getName()` method from the `Cabbie` object. In effect, the supervisor is asking the cabbie for its name (see Figure 5.2).

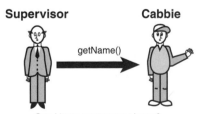

Supervisor **Cabbie**

getName()

Can I have your name please?

FIGURE 5.2

The public interface specifies how the objects interact.

Users of your code need to know nothing about its internal workings. All they need to know is how to create and use the object. Give them a way to get in, but hide the details.

Hiding the Implementation

The need for hiding the implementation has been covered in great detail. Whereas identifying the public interface is a design issue that revolves around the users of the class, the implementation should not involve the users at all. Of course, the implementation must provide the services that the user needs, but how these services are actually performed should not be known to the user. A class is most useful if the implementation can change without affecting the users. In short, a change to the implementation should not necessitate a change in application code.

In the cabbie example, the `Cabbie` class may have behavior pertaining to how it eats breakfast. However, the cabbie's supervisor does not need to know what the cabbie has for breakfast. Thus, this behavior is part of the implementation of the `Cabbie` object and should not be available to other objects in this system (see Figure 5.3). Gilbert and McCarty, in their book *Object-Oriented Design in Java*, on page 128, state that the prime directive of encapsulation is that *all fields shall be private*. In this way, none of the fields in a class is accessible from other objects.

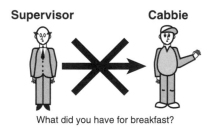

FIGURE 5.3
Objects don't need to know some implementation details.

Designing Robust Constructors (and Perhaps Destructors)

When designing a class, one of the most important design issues involves how the class will be constructed. Constructors are discussed in Chapter 3, "Advanced Object-Oriented Concepts." Revisit this discussion if you need a refresher on guidelines for designing constructors.

First and foremost, a constructor should put an object into a safe state. This includes issues such as attribute initialization and memory management. In his book *Effective C++*, on page 34, Scott Meyers discusses some of these issues in the section "Constructors, Destructors and

Assignment Operators." You also need to make sure the object is constructed properly in the default condition. It is normally a good idea to provide a constructor to handle this default situation.

In languages that include destructors, it is of vital importance that the destructors include clean-up functions properly. In most cases, this clean-up pertains to releasing system memory that the object acquired at some point. Java reclaims memory automatically with a garbage collection mechanism. In languages such as C++, the developer must include code in the destructor to properly free up the memory that the object acquired during its existence. If this function is ignored, a memory leak will result.

WARNING

When an object fails to properly release the memory that it acquired during an object's life cycle, then the memory is lost to the entire operating system as long as the application that created the object is executing. For example, suppose multiple objects of the same class are created and then destroyed, perhaps in some sort of loop. If these objects fail to release their memory when they go out of scope, this memory leak slowly depletes the available pool of system memory. At some point, it is possible that enough memory will be consumed that the system will have no available memory left to allocate. This means that any application executing in the system would be unable to acquire any memory. This could put the application in an unsafe state and even lock up the system.

Designing Error Handling into a Class

As with the design of constructors, designing how a class handles errors is of vital importance. Error handling is discussed in detail in Chapter 3. Revisit this discussion to brush up on designing ~~constructors~~. *error handling.*

It is almost certain that every system will encounter unforeseen problems. Thus, it is not a good idea to simply ignore potential errors. The developer of a good class (or any code, for that matter) anticipates potential errors and includes code to handle these conditions when they are encountered.

The rule of thumb is that the application should never crash. When an error is encountered, the system should either fix itself and continue, or exit gracefully without losing any data that's important to the user.

Documenting a Class and Using Comments

In every book and article, in every code review, in every discussion you have about good design, the topic of comments and documentation comes up. Unfortunately, comments and good documentation are often not taken seriously or, even worse, they are ignored.

Most developers know that they should thoroughly document their code, but they don't usually want to take the time to do it. The bottom line is that a good design is practically impossible without good documentation practices. At the class level, the scope may be small enough that a developer can get away with shoddy documentation. However, when the class gets passed to someone else to extend and/or maintain, or it becomes part of a larger system (which is what should happen), then a lack of proper documentation and comments can be lethal.

All this has been said before by many people. One of the most crucial aspects of a good design, whether it's a design for a class or something else, is to carefully document the process.

Building Objects with the Intent to Cooperate

In Chapter 6, "Designing with Objects: The Software Design Process," we discuss the issues involved in designing a system. We can safely say that almost no class lives in isolation. In most cases there is no reason to build a class if it is not going to interact with other classes. This is simply a fact in the life of a class. The class will service other classes, it will request the services of other classes, or both. In later chapters we will discuss various ways that classes interact with each other.

In the cabbie example, the cabbie and the supervisor are not standalone entities; they interact with each other at various levels (see Figure 5.4).

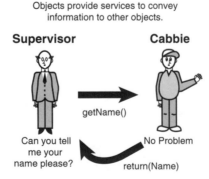

FIGURE 5.4
Objects should request information.

When designing a class, make sure that you are aware of how other objects will interact with it.

Designing with Reuse in Mind

Objects can be reused in different systems, and code should be written with reuse in mind. For example, when a Cabbie class is developed and tested, it can be used anywhere you need a cabbie. To make a class usable in various systems, the class must be designed with reuse in mind. This is where much of the thought is required in the design process. Attempting to figure out all the possible scenarios in which a Cabbie object must operate is not a trivial task.

Designing with Extensibility in Mind

Adding new features to a class may be as easy as extending an existing class, and adding a few new methods and modifying the behavior of others. It is not necessary to rewrite everything. This is where inheritance comes into play. If you have just written a Person class, you must consider the fact that you may later want to write an Employee class, or a Vendor class. Thus, having Employee inherit from Person may be the best strategy; in this case, the Person class is said to be *extensible*. You do not want to design Person so that it contains behavior that prevents it from being extended by classes such as Employee or Vendor (assuming, of course, that in your design you really intend for other classes to extend Person).

This point touches on the abstraction guideline discussed earlier. Person should contain only the data and behaviors that are specific to a person. Other classes can then subclass it and inherit appropriate data and behaviors.

> ### What Attributes and Methods Can Be Static?
> It is important to decide what attributes and methods can be declared as static. Revisit the discussions in Chapter 3 on using the static keyword to understand how to design these into your classes.

Making Names Descriptive

Earlier we discussed the use of proper documentation and comments. Following a naming convention for your classes, attributes, and methods is a similar subject. There are many naming conventions, and the convention you choose is not as important as choosing one and sticking to it. However, when you choose a convention, make sure that when you create classes, attributes, and method names, you not only follow the convention, but make the names descriptive. When someone reads the name, he or she should be able to tell from the name what the object represents.

> ## Good Naming
>
> Make sure that a naming convention makes sense. As already stated, there are many possible naming conventions. Often, people go overboard and create conventions that may make sense to them, but are totally incomprehensible to others. Take care when forcing other to conform to a convention. Make sure that the conventions are sensible and that everyone involved understands the intent behind them.

Making names descriptive is a good development practice that applies to more than just O-O development.

Abstracting Out Non-portable Code

If you are designing a system that must use nonportable code (that is, the code will only run on a specific hardware platform), then you should abstract this code out of the class. By abstracting out, we mean isolating the non-portable code in its own class. For example, if you are writing code to access a serial port, you should create a wrapper class to deal with this code. Then, your class should send a message to the wrapper class to get the information or services it needs. Do not put the system-dependent code into your primary class (see Figure 5.5).

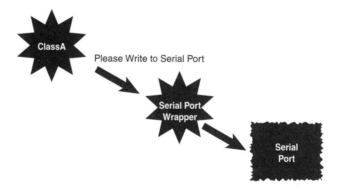

FIGURE 5.5
A serial port wrapper.

If the class moves to another hardware system, the way to access the serial port changes, or you want to go to a parallel port, the code in your primary class does not have to change. The only place the code needs to change is in the wrapper class.

Providing a Way to Copy and Compare Objects

Chapter 3 discusses the issue of copying and comparing objects. It is important to understand how objects are copied and compared. You may not want, or expect, a simple bitwise copy or compare operation. You must make sure that your class behaves as expected, and this means you have to spend some time designing how objects are copied and compared.

Keeping the Scope as Small as Possible

Keeping the scope as small as possible goes hand-in-hand with abstraction and hiding the implementation. The idea is to localize attributes and behaviors as much as possible. In this way, maintaining, testing, and extending a class are much easier.

> ### Keeping Scope as Small as Possible
> Minimizing the scope of global variables is a good programming style, and not specific to O-O programming.

For example, if you have a method that requires a temporary attribute, keep it local. Consider the following code:

```
public class Math {

    int temp=0;

    public int swap (int a, int b) {

        temp = a;
        a=b;
        b=temp;

        return temp;

    }

}
```

What is wrong with this class? The problem is that the attribute `temp` is only needed within the scope of the `swap()` method. There is no reason for it to be at the class level. Thus, you should move `temp` within the scope of the `swap()` method:

```
public class Math {

    public int swap (int a, int b) {
```

5

```
        int temp=0;

        temp = a;
        a=b;
        b=temp;

        return temp;

    }

}
```

This is what is meant by keeping the scope as small as possible.

A Class Should Be Responsible for Itself

In a training class based on their book, *Java Primer Plus*, by Tyma, Torok and Downing, the authors propose the class design guideline that all objects should be responsible for acting on themselves whenever possible. Consider trying to print a circle.

First, let's use a non-O-O example. The print command finds `Circle` and prints it (see Figure 5.6):

```
Print(circle);
```

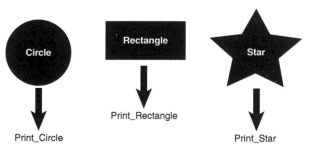

Choose a Shape and Print

FIGURE 5.6

A non-O-O example of a Print scenario.

`Print`, `Draw`, and other functions need to have a case statement (or something like an `if/else` structure) to determine what to do for the given shape passed. In this case, a separate print routine for each shape could be called.

Every time you add a new shape, all the functions need to add the shape to their `case` statement.

Now let's look at an O-O example. By using polymorphism and grouping the `Circle` into a `Shape` category, `Shape` figures out that it is a `Circle` and knows how to print itself (see Figure 5.7):

```
Shape.print(); // Shape is actually a Circle
```

A Shape Knows How to Print Itself

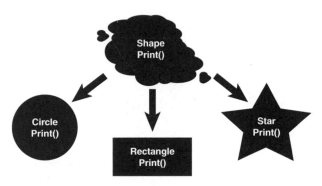

FIGURE 5.7
An O-O example of a Print scenario.

Serializing and Marshalling Objects

We have already discussed the problem of using objects in environments that were originally designed for structured programming. The middleware example, where we wrote objects to a relational database, is one good example. We also touched on the problem of writing an object to a flat file or sending it over a network.

Basically, to send an object over a wire (for example, to a file, over a network), the system must deconstruct the object (that is, flatten it out), send it over the wire, and then reconstruct it on the other end of the wire. This process is called *serializing* an object. (For an in-depth discussion on object serialization, reference the book *Java 1.1 Developers Guide,* page 933, by Jamie Jaworski.) The act of actually sending the object across a wire is called *marshalling* an object. A serialized object, in theory, can be written to a flat file and retrieved later, in the same state in which it was written.

The major issue here is that the serialization and deserialization must use the same specifications. It is sort of like an encryption algorithm. If one object encrypts a string, then the object that wants to decrypt it must use the same encryption algorithm. Java provides an interface called `Serializable` that provides this translation.

Designing with Maintainability in Mind

Designing useful and concise classes promotes a high level of maintainability. Just as you design a class with extensibility in mind, you should also design with future maintenance in mind.

The process of designing classes forces you to organize your code into many hopefully manageable pieces. Separate pieces of code tend to be more maintainable than larger pieces of code (at least that's the idea). One of the best ways to promote maintainability is to reduce interdependent code—that is, changes in one class have no or minimal effects on other classes.

Highly Coupled Classes

Classes that are highly dependent on one another are considered *highly coupled*. Thus, if a change made to one class forces a change to another class, these two classes are considered highly coupled. Classes that have no such dependencies have a very low degree of coupling (for more information on coupling, reference the book *The Object Primer,* on page 148, by Scott Ambler).

This means that changes should only be made to the implementation of an object. Changes to the public interface should be avoided at all costs. Any changes to the public interface will cause ripple effects throughout all the systems that utilize the interface.

For example, if a change were made to the `getName()` method of the `Cabbie` class, then every single place in all systems that use this interface must be changed and recompiled. Simply finding all these method calls is a daunting task.

To promote a high level of maintainability, keep the coupling level of your classes as low as possible.

Using Object Persistence

Object persistence is another issue that must be addressed in many O-O systems. *Persistence* is the concept of maintaining the state of an object. When you run a program, if you don't save the object in some manner, then the object simply dies, never to be recovered. These transient objects may work in some applications, but in most business systems, the state of the object must be saved for later use. In his book *The Object Primer*, on page 133, Scott Ambler devotes an entire section to this topic.

In its simplest form, an object can persist by being serialized and written to a flat file. While it is true that an object theoretically can persist in memory as long as it is not destroyed, we will concentrate on storing persistent objects on some sort of storage device. There are three primary storage devices to consider:

- Flat file system—You can store an object in a flat file by serializing the object. This has very limited use.
- Relational database—Some sort of middleware is necessary to convert an object to a relational model.
- O-O database—This is the logical way to make objects persistent, but most companies have all their data in legacy systems and are just starting to explore object databases. Even brand-new O-O applications must usually interface with legacy data.

Using Iteration

As in most design and programming functions, using an iterative process is recommended. This dovetails well into the concept of providing minimal interfaces. A good testing plan quickly uncovers any areas where insufficient interfaces are provided. In this way, the process can iterate until the class has the appropriate interfaces. This testing process is not simply confined to coding. Testing the design with walkthroughs and other design review techniques is very helpful. Testers' lives are more pleasant when iterative processes are used because they are involved in the process early and are not simply handed a system that is thrown over the wall at the end of the development process.

Testing the Interface

The minimal implementations of the interface are often called *stubs*. (Gilbert and McCarty have a good discussion on stubs in their book *Object-Oriented Design in Java*.) By using stubs you can test the interfaces without writing any *real* code. In the following example, rather than connect to an actual database, stubs are used to verify that the interfaces are working properly (from the users perspective—remember that the interfaces are meant for the user). Thus, the implementation is really not necessary at this point. In fact, it may cost valuable time and energy to complete the implementation at this point because the design of the interface will affect the implementation, and the interface is not yet complete.

In Figure 5.8, note that when a user class sends a message to the DataBaseReader class, the information returned to the user class is provided by code stubs, and not by the actual database (in fact the database most likely does not exist yet). When the interface is complete and the implementation is under development, then the database can be connected and the stubs disconnected.

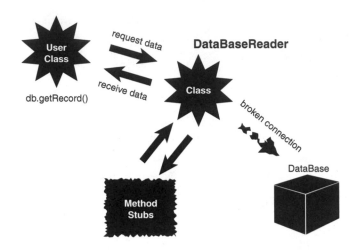

FIGURE 5.8
Using stubs.

Here is a code example that uses an internal array to simulate a working database (albeit a simple one):

```
public class DataBaseReader {

    String db[] = { "Record1",
        "Record2",
        "Record3",
        "Record4",
        "Record5"};

    boolean DBOpen = false;
    int pos;

    public void open(String Name){
        DBOpen = true;
    };
    public void close(){
        DBOpen = false;
    };
    public void goToFirst(){
        pos = 0;
    };
    public void goToLast(){
        pos = 4;
    };
```

```
public int howManyRecords(){
    int numOfRecords = 5;

    return numOfRecords;
};
public String getRecord(int key){

    /* DB Specific Implementation */
    return db[key];
};
public String getNextRecord(){

    /* DB Specific Implementation */
    return db[pos++];
};

}
```

Notice how the methods simulate the database calls. The strings within the array represent the records that will be written to the database. When the database is successfully integrated into the system, then it will be substituted for the array.

Keeping the Stubs Around

When you are done with the stubs, don't delete them. Keep them in the code for possible later use. In fact, in a well-designed program, your test stubs should be integrated into the design and kept in the program for later use. In short, design the testing right into the class!

As you find problems with the interface design, make changes and repeat the process until you are satisfied with the result.

Conclusion

This chapter presents many guidelines that can help you in designing classes. This is by no means a complete list of guidelines. You will undoubtedly come across additional guidelines as you go about your travels in O-O design.

This chapter deals with design issues as they pertain to individual classes. However, we have already seen that a class does not live in isolation. Classes must be designed to interact with other classes. A group of classes that interact with each other is part of a system. Ultimately, these systems provide value to end users. Chapter 6 covers the topic of designing complete systems.

5

References

Gilbert, Stephen, and Bill McCarty: *Object-Oriented Design in Java*. The Waite Group, 1998.

Meyers, Scott: *Effective C++*. Addison-Wesley, 1992.

Tyma, Paul, Gabriel Torok and Troy Downing: *Java Primer Plus*. The Waite Group, 1996.

Ambler, Scott: *The Object Primer.* Cambridge University Press, 1998.

Jaworski, Jamie: *Java 1.1 Developers Guide.* Sams Publishing, 1997.

Designing with Objects: The Software Development Process

IN THIS CHAPTER

- Learn about the object-oriented design process

- Start the process of finding classes

- Learn how to start the process of identifying responsibilities and collaborations

When you use a software product, you expect it to behave as advertised. Unfortunately, not all products live up to expectations. The problem is that when most products are produced, the majority of time and effort go into the engineering phase, and not enough go into the design phase.

Object-oriented (O-O) design has been touted as a robust and flexible software development approach. The truth is that you can create a very bad O-O design just as easily as you can create a very bad non–O-O design. Don't be lulled into a sense of security just because you are using a *state-of-the-art* O-O design tool. You have to pay attention to the design and invest the proper time and effort into it in order to create the best product.

Design Guidelines

While chapter 5, "Class Design Guidelines," concentrated on designing good classes, this chapter focuses on designing good systems (a system can be considered as classes that interact with each other). Proper design practices have evolved throughout the history of software development, and there is no reason you should not take advantage of the blood, sweat, and tears of your software predecessors, whether they used O-O technologies or not.

One fallacy is that there is one *true* design methodology. This is not the case. There is no right or wrong way to create a design. There are many design methodologies available today, and they all have their proponents. However, the primary issue is not which design method to use, but simply whether to use a method at all. This can be expanded to the entire software development process. Many organizations do not follow a standard software development process. The most important factor in creating a good design is to find a process that you and your organization can feel comfortable with. It makes no sense to implement a design process that no one will follow.

Most books that deal with object-oriented technologies offer very similar strategies for designing systems. In fact, except for some of the object-oriented specific issues involved, much of the strategy is applicable to non–object-oriented systems as well.

Generally, a solid O-O design process will include the following steps:

- Doing the proper analysis
- Developing a statement of work that describes the system
- Gathering the requirements from this statement of work
- Developing a prototype for the user interface
- Identifying the classes
- Determining the responsibilities of each class
- Determining how the various classes interact with each other
- Creating a high-level model that describes the system to be built

Although the entire process is obviously important, this book is especially interested in the last item in this list: the system model, which is made up of class diagrams and class interactions. This model should represent the system faithfully and be easy to understand and modify. We also need a notation for the model. This is where The Unified Modeling Language (UML) comes in. As you know, the UML is not a design process, but a modeling language.

The Ongoing Design Process

Despite the best intentions and planning, in all but the most trivial cases, the design is an ongoing process. Even after a product is in testing, design changes will pop up. It is up to the project manager to draw the line that says when to stop changing a product and adding features.

It is important to understand that many design methodologies are available. One methodology, called the waterfall model, advocates strict boundaries between the various phases. In this case, the design phase is completed before the implementation phase, which is completed before the testing phase, etc. In practice, the waterfall model has been found to be unrealistic. Currently there are other design models, such as rapid prototyping, that promote a true iterative process. In these models, some implementation is attempted prior to completing the design phase as a type of proof-of-concept. Despite the recent aversion to the waterfall model, the goal behind the model is understandable. Doing a complete and thorough design before starting to code is a sound practice. You do not want to be in the release phase of the product and then deciding to iterate through the design phase again. Iterating across phase boundaries is unavoidable; however, you should keep these iterations to a minimum (see Figure 6.1).

Simply put, the reason to identify requirements early and keep design changes to a minimum are as follows:

- The cost of a requirement/design change in the design phase is relatively small.
- The cost of a design change in the implementation phase is significantly higher.
- The cost of a design change in the deployment phase is astronomical.

Similarly, you would not want the construction of your dream house to be initiated until the architect had completed the drawings. This statement seems ridiculous to most people. In fact, if I said that the Golden Gate Bridge or the Empire State Building were constructed without any design, you would find the statement absolutely crazy. Yet, you would most likely not find it crazy if I told you that the software you were using might not have had a thorough design, and in fact, it might not have been thoroughly tested.

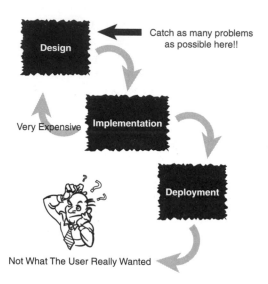

FIGURE 6.1
Catching problems as early as possible.

That said, it may well be impossible to thoroughly test software. But that does not mean that we should not try. Bridges and software may not be directly comparable; however, software must strive for the same level of engineering excellence as the "harder" engineering disciplines such as bridge building. Poor-quality software can kill people; it's not just wrong numbers on payroll checks. For example, inferior software in medical equipment can kill and maim people.

Safety Versus Economics

Would you want to cross a bridge that has not been inspected and tested? It is unfortunately the case with many software packages, the users are left with the responsibility to do the majority of the testing. This is very costly for both the users and the software provider. Unfortunately, short-term economics often seems to be the primary factor in making project decisions.

Since customers seem to be willing to pay the price and put up with software of poor quality, software providers find that it is cheaper in the long run to let the customers test the product rather than do it themselves. In the short term this may be true, but in the long run it costs far more than the software provider realizes. Ultimately, the software provider's reputation will be damaged.

Some major computer software companies are infamous for using the beta test phase to let the customers do testing—testing that should have been done before the beta even reached the customer. Although this strategy damages the company's reputation, many customers are willing to take the risk of using prerelease software simply because they are anxious to get the functionality the product promises.

After the software is released, problems that have not been caught and fixed prior to release become much more expensive. To illustrate, consider the dilemma automobile companies face when they are confronted with a recall. If a defect in the automobile is identified and fixed before it is shipped (hopefully before it is manufactured), it is much cheaper than if all delivered automobiles have to be recalled and fixed one at a time. Not only is this scenario very expensive, but it damages the reputation of the company. In an increasingly competitive market, high-quality software, support services, and reputation are *the* competitive advantage (see Figure 6.2).

WARNING

Although it may be acceptable to compare automobiles, bridges, and software when discussing quality, the legal implications of these topics cannot be compared, at least not yet. The legal issues regarding software are currently being defined and revised. Currently disclaimers such as "we are responsible for nothing that this software does or causes to happen" abound. Some other industries do not have this luxury. As the software legal process evolves and matures, software manufacturers may well have to contend with these issues. (As a standard disclaimer, in no way does this book attempt to offer any legal advice.)

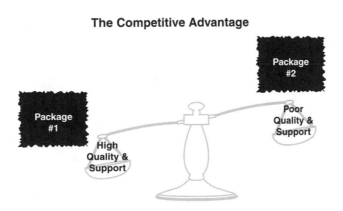

The Competitive Advantage

FIGURE 6.2

The competitive advantage.

The following sections provide brief summaries of the items listed previously as being part of the design process. Later in the chapter we will work through an example that explains in greater detail each of these items.

Doing the Proper Analysis

There are a lot of variables involved in doing a design and creating a software product. The users must work hand-in-hand with the developers at all stages. In the analysis phase the users and the developers must do the proper research and analysis to determine the statement of work, the requirements of the project, and whether to actually do the project. The third point may seem a bit surprising, but it is important. During the analysis phase, there must not be any hesitation to terminate the project if there is a valid reason to do so. Too many times, a pet project, or some political inertia, keeps a project going, regardless of the obvious warning signs that cry out for project cancellation. Assuming that the project is viable, the primary focus of the analysis phase is for everyone to learn the systems (both the old and the proposed new one) and determine the system requirements.

Developing a Statement of Work

The *statement of work* is a text document that describes the system. Although determining the requirements is the ultimate goal of the analysis phase, requirements are not in a format that a nondeveloper usually sees. The statement of work is a document that should give anyone who reads it a complete understanding of the system. Regardless of how it is written, the statement of work must represent the complete system and be clear about how the system will look and feel.

The statement of work contains everything that must be known about the system. Many customers create a request-for-proposal (RFP) to a vendor, which is similar to the statement of work. A customer creates an RFP that totally describes the system they want built and sends it to multiple vendors. The vendors then use this document, and whatever analysis they need to do, to determine whether they should bid on the project and, if so, what price to charge.

Gathering the Requirements

The requirements document describes what the users want the system to do. Even though the level of detail of the requirements document does not need to be of a highly technical nature, the requirements must be specific enough to represent the true nature of the user's needs for the end product. The requirements document must be of sufficient detail for the user to make educated judgments about the completeness of the system. It must also be of specific detail for a design group to use the document to proceed with the design phase.

Whereas the statement of work is a document written in paragraph form, the requirements are usually represented as a summary statement or presented as bulleted items. Each individual bulleted item represents one specific requirement of the system. The requirements are distilled from the statement of work. This process is shown later in the chapter.

In many ways, these requirements are the most important part of the system. The statement of work may contain irrelevant material; however, the requirements are the final representation of the system that must be implemented. All future documents in the software development process will be based on the requirements.

Developing a Prototype of the User Interface

One of the best ways to make sure users and developers understand the system is to create a prototype. A prototype can be just about anything; however, most people consider the proto-type to be a simulated user interface. By creating actual screens and screen flows, it is easier for people to get an idea of what they will be working with and what the system will feel like. In any event, a prototype will almost certainly not contain all the functionality of the final sys-tem.

Most prototypes are created with an integrated development environment (IDE). However, drawing the screens on a whiteboard or even on paper may be all that is needed. Visual Basic is a good environment for prototyping. Remember that you are not necessarily creating busi-ness logic (the logic/code behind the interface that actually does the work) when you build the prototype, although it is possible to do so. The look and feel of the user interface are the major concerns at this point. Having a good prototype can help immensely when finding classes.

Identifying the Classes

After the requirements are recorded, the process of identifying classes can begin. From the requirements, one way of identifying classes is to highlight all the nouns. These are objects, such as people, places, and things. Don't be too fussy about getting all the classes right the first time. You might end up eliminating classes, adding classes, and changing classes at various stages throughout the design. It is important to get something down first. Take advantage of the fact that the design is an iterative process. As in other forms of brainstorming, get something down initially, with the understanding that the final result might look nothing like the initial pass.

Determining the Responsibilities of Each Class

You need to determine the responsibilities of each class you have identified. What must the class store and what operations must it perform? For example, an `Employee` object would be responsible for calculating payroll and transferring the money to the appropriate account. It might also be responsible for storing the various payroll rates and the account numbers of various banks.

Determining How the Classes Interact with Each Other

Most classes do not exist in isolation. Although a class must fulfill certain responsibilities, many times it will have to interact with another class to get something that it wants. This is where the messages between classes come in. One class can send a message to another class when it needs information from that class or if it wants the other class to do something for it.

Creating a Class Model to Describe the System

When all the classes are determined and the class responsibilities and collaborations are listed, a class model that represents the complete system can be built. The class model shows how the various classes interact within the system.

In this book, we are using UML to model the system. Several tools on the market use UML and provide a good environment for creating and maintaining UML class models. Some of these products include Rational Rose and TogetherJ. As we develop the example in the next section, we will see how the class diagrams fit into the big picture and how modeling large systems would be virtually impossible without some sort of good modeling notation and modeling tool.

A Blackjack Example

The rest of this chapter is dedicated to a case study pertaining to the design process covered in the previous sections. Walking through a case study seems to be a standard exercise in many object-oriented books that deal with O-O design.

My first recollection of such an exercise was a graduate course that I took where we followed an example in the book *Designing Object-Oriented Software*, by Wrifs-Brock, Wilkerson, and Weiner. In this book, the case study was that of an automated teller system (ATM). The iterative process of identifying the classes and responsibilities using CRC modeling was an eye-opening experience. The books *The Object Primer*, by Scott Ambler, and *Object-Oriented Design in Java*, by Gilbert and McCarty, both go through similar exercises using CRC modeling and Use Cases.

Let's start an example that we will expand on throughout this chapter.

Because we want to have some fun, instead of creating a payroll system, ATM systems or something of the like, let's create a program that simulates a game of blackjack. We will assume that the statement of work has already been completed. In fact, let's say that a

Designing with Objects: The Software Development Process

CHAPTER 6

105

6

THE SOFTWARE
DEVELOPMENT
PROCESS

customer has come to you with a proposal that includes a very well-written statement of work and a rule book about how to play blackjack.

According to the statement of work, the basic goal is to design a software system that will simulate the game of blackjack (see Figure 6.3). Remember, we will not describe how to implement this game—we are only going to design the system. Ultimately, this will culminate in the discovery of the classes, along with their responsibilities and collaborations. After some intense analysis, we have determined the requirements of the system. In this case we will use a requirements summary statement; however, we could have presented the requirements as bullets. Since this is a small system, a requirements summary statement may make more sense. However, in most large systems, a database of the requirements (in bulleted list format) would be more appropriate. Here is the requirements summary statement:

FIGURE 6.3
A winning blackjack hand.

Requirements Summary Statement

The intended purpose of this software application is to implement a game of blackjack. In the game of blackjack one or more individuals play against the dealer (or house). Although there may be more than one player, each player plays only against the dealer, and not any of the other players.

From a player's perspective, the goal of the game is to draw cards from the deck until the sum of the face value of all the cards equals 21 or as close to 21 as possible, without exceeding 21. If the sum of the face value of all the cards exceeds 21, then the player loses. If the sum of the face value of the first two cards equals 21, then the player is said to have blackjack.

continues

Requirements Summary Statement

The dealer plays the game along with the players. The dealer must deal the cards, present a player with additional cards, show all or part of a hand, calculate the value of all or part of a hand, calculate the number of cards in a hand, determine the winner, and start a new hand.

A card must know what its face value is and be able to report this value. The suit of the card is of no importance (but it might be for another game in the future). All cards must be members of a deck of cards. This deck must have the functionality to deal the next card, as well as report how many cards remain in the deck.

During the game, a player can request that a card be dealt to his or her hand. The player must be able to display the hand, calculate the face value of the hand, and determine the number of cards in the hand. When the dealer asks the player whether to deal another card or to start a new game, the player must respond.

Each card has its own face value (suit does not factor into the face value). Aces count as 1 or 11. Face cards (Jack, Queen, King) each count as 10. The rest of the cards represent their face values.

The rules of the game state that if the sum of the face value of the player's cards is closer to 21 than the sum of the face value of the dealer's cards, the player wins an amount equal to the bet that was made. If the player wins with a blackjack, then the player wins 3:2 times the bet made (assuming that the dealer does not also have blackjack). If the sum of the face value of the player's cards exceeds 21, then the bet is lost. Blackjack (an ace and a face card or a 10) beats other combinations of 21.

If the player and the dealer have identical scores and at least 17, then it is considered a draw and the player retains the bet.

As already mentioned, you could also have presented the requirements in bullet form, as we did for the `DataBaseReader` class in Chapter 2, "How to Think in Terms of Objects."

We want to take the perspective of the user. Since we are not interested in the implementation, we'll concentrate on the interface. Think back to the black-box example from Chapter 1, "What an Object Really Is." We only care about *what* the system does, not *how* it does it.

The next step is to study the requirements summary statement and start identifying the classes. Before we actually start this process, let's define how we are going to model and track the classes that we ultimately identify.

Using CRC Cards

Discovering classes is not a trivial process. In the blackjack example we are working on, there will be relatively few classes because this is intended as an example. However, in most business systems there could be dozens of classes—perhaps 100 or more. There must be a way to

Designing with Objects: The Software Development Process

CHAPTER 6

107

6

THE SOFTWARE
DEVELOPMENT
PROCESS

keep track of the classes as well as their interactions. One of the most popular methods for identifying and categorizing classes is to use class-responsibility-collaboration (CRC) cards. Each CRC card represents a single class's data attributes, responsibilities, and collaborations.

One of the more endearing qualities of CRC cards is that they are non-electronic (although I'm sure that there are computer applications around that simulate CRC cards). CRC cards are, quite literally, a collection of standard index cards.

You need to create three sections on each card:

- The name of the class
- The responsibilities of the class
- The collaborations of the class

The use of CRC cards conjures up scenes of dimly lit rooms, partially filled boxes of pizza, pop cans, and multitudes of index cards strewn around the room. While this may be partially true, using CRC cards is a good technique because many of the people involved with the design will not be developers. They may not even have much computer experience. Thus, using the index cards to discover classes is a technique that everyone can understand. Figure 6.4 shows the format of a CRC card.

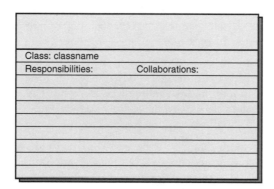

FIGURE 6.4
The format of a CRC card.

Identifying the Blackjack Classes

Remember that, in general, classes correspond to nouns, which are objects—people, places, and things. If you go through the requirements summary statement and highlight all the nouns, then you have a good list from which you can start gleaning your objects.

As stated earlier, you shouldn't get too hung up in getting things right the first time. Not all the classes that you identify from the list of nouns, or elsewhere, will make it through to the final cut. On the other hand, there may be some classes that do make the final cut that were not in your original list. Start feeling comfortable with the iterative process throughout the design. And as always, make sure that you realize that there are always many ways to skin a cat. We have already stated that if you put 10 people in different rooms, they will come up with 10 different designs, and they might all be equally good. In most cases, although the designs may be different, hopefully there will be significant overlap. Of course, when working with a team, the final design will have to be a consensus, iterating and evolving to a common solution.

Let's identify some nouns from our blackjack example:

> The intended purpose of this software application is to implement a **game** of **blackjack**. In the game of blackjack one or more **individuals** play against the **dealer** (or **house**). Although there may be more than one **player**, each player plays only against the **dealer**, and not any of the other **players**.

> From a **player's** perspective, the goal of the **game** is to draw **cards** from the **deck** until the sum of the **face value** of all the **cards** equals 21 or as close to 21 as possible, without exceeding 21. If the sum of the **face value** of all the **cards** exceeds 21, then the **player** loses. If the sum of the **face value** of the first two **cards** equals 21, then the **player** is said to have blackjack.

> The **dealer** plays the **game** along with the **players**. The **dealer** must deal the **cards**, present a **player** with additional **cards**, show all or part of a **hand**, calculate the value of all or part of a **hand**, calculate the number of cards in a **hand**, determine the **winner**, and start a new **hand**.

> A **card** must know what its **face value** is and be able to report this value. The suit of the **card** is of no importance (but it might be for another game in the future). All **cards** must be members of a **deck** of **cards**. This **deck** must have the functionality to deal the next **card**, as well as report how many **cards** remain in the deck.

> During the **game**, a **player** can request that a **card** be dealt to his or her **hand**. The **player** must be able to display the **hand**, calculate the **face value** of the **hand**, and determine the number of **cards** in the **hand**. When the **dealer** asks the **player** whether to deal another **card** or to start a new **game**, the **player** must respond.

Designing with Objects: The Software Development Process

CHAPTER 6

109

6

THE SOFTWARE
DEVELOPMENT
PROCESS

Each **card** has its own **face value** (**suit** does not factor into the **face value**). Aces count as 1 or 11. **Face cards** (**Jack**, **Queen**, **King**) each count as 10. The rest of the **cards** represent their **face values**.

The rules of the **game** state that if the sum of the **face value** of the **player's cards** is closer to 21 than the sum of the **face value** of the **dealer's cards**, the player wins an amount equal to the **bet** that was made. If the **player** wins with a blackjack, then the **player** wins 3:2 times the **bet** made (assuming that the **dealer** does not also have **blackjack**). If the sum of the **face value** of the **player's cards** exceeds 21, then the **bet** is lost. **Blackjack** (an ace and a face card or a 10) beats other combinations of 21.

If the **player** and the **dealer** have identical scores and at least 17, then it is considered a draw and the player retains the bet.

Now let's make a list of the possible objects(classes):

- Game
- Blackjack
- Dealer
- House
- Players
- Player
- Cards
- Card
- Deck
- Hand
- Face value
- Suit
- Winner
- Ace
- Face card
- King
- Queen
- Game
- Bet

Can you find any other possible classes that were missed? There may well be some classes that you feel should be in the list but are not. There may also be classes that you feel should not have made the list. In any event, we now have a starting point and we can begin the process of fine-tuning the list of classes. This is an iterative process and although we have 19 potential classes, our final class list may be a lot shorter.

Again, remember that this is just the initial pass. You will want to iterate through this a number of times and make changes. You may even find that you left an important object out or that you need to split one object into two objects. Now let's explore each of the possible classes:

- Game—**blackjack** is the name of the game. Thus, we will treat this in the same way we treated the noun *game*.

- ~~Blackjack~~—In this case **game** may be considered a noun, but the game is actually the system itself, so we will eliminate this as a potential class.

- Dealer—Because we cannot do without a dealer, we will keep this one (as a note, we could abstract out the stuff pertaining to people in general, but we won't in this example). It may also be possible to avoid a dealer class altogether, thus having the dealer simply be an instance of the player class. However, there are enough additional attributes of a dealer that we should probably keep this class.

- ~~House~~—This one is easy because it is just another name for the dealer, so we strike it.

- ~~Players~~ and player—We need players, so we have to have this class. However, we want the class to represent a single player and not a group of players, so we strike players and keep player.

- ~~Cards~~ and card—This one follows the same logic as player. We absolutely need cards in the game, but we want the class to represent a single card, so we strike cards and keep card.

- Deck—Because there are a lot of actions required by a deck (like shuffling and drawing), we decide that this is a good choice for a class.

- Hand—This class represents a gray area. Each player will have a hand. In this game, we will require that a player has a single hand. So it would be possible for a player to keep track of the cards without having to have a hand object. However, because it is theoretically possible for a player to have multiple hands and because we may want to use the concept of a hand in other card games, we will keep this class. Remember that one of the goals of a design is to be extensible. If we create a good design for the blackjack game, then perhaps we can reuse the classes later for other card games.

- ~~Face value~~—The face value of the card is best represented as an attribute in the card class, so let's strike class.

- ~~Suit~~—Again, this is a gray area. For the blackjack game we do not need to keep track of the suit. However, there are card games that need to keep track of the suit. Thus, to make this class reusable, we should track it. However, the suit is not a good candidate for a class. It should be an attribute of a card, so we will strike it as a class.

- ~~Ace~~—This could better be represented as an attribute of the card class, so let's strike it as a class.
- ~~Royal Card~~—This could better be represented as attribute of the card class, so let's strike it as a class.
- ~~King~~—This could better be represented as attribute of the card class, so let's strike it as a class.
- ~~Queen~~—This could better be represented as attribute of the card class, so let's strike it as a class.
- Bet—This class presents a dilemma. Technically you could play blackjack without a bet; however, the requirements statement clearly includes a bet in the description. The bet could be considered an attribute of the player in this case, but there are many other games where a player does not need to have a bet. In short, a bet is not a logical attribute of a player. Also, abstracting out the bet is a good idea because we may want to bet various things. You can bet money, chips, your watch, your horse, or even the title to your house. Even though there may be many valid arguments not to make the bet a class, in this case we will.

We are left with six classes, as shown in Figure 6.5.

BackJack Game

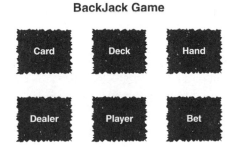

| Card | Deck | Hand |
| Dealer | Player | Bet |

FIGURE 6.5
The initial blackjack classes

Identifying the Classes' Responsibilities

Responsibilities relate to actions. You can generally identify responsibilities by selecting the verbs from the summary of the requirements. From this list you can glean your responsibilities. However, keep in mind the following:

- Not all verbs in the requirements summary will ultimately end up as responsibilities.
- You might need to combine several verbs to find an actual responsibility.
- Some responsibilities ultimately chosen will not be in the original requirements summary.
- Because this is an iterative process, you need to keep revising and updating both the requirements summary and the responsibilities.
- If two or more classes share a responsibility, then each class will have the responsibility.

Let's take an initial stab at identifying the verbs, which will lead us down the path toward uncovering the responsibilities of our classes:

The intended purpose of this software application is to **implement** a game of blackjack. In the game of blackjack one or more individuals **play** against the dealer (or house). Although there may be more than one player, each player **plays** only against the dealer, and not any of the other players.

From a player's perspective, the goal of the game is to **draw** cards from the deck until the sum of the face value of all the cards equals 21 or as close to 21 as possible, without exceeding 21. If the sum of the face value of all the cards exceeds 21, then the player **loses**. If the sum of the face value of the first two cards equals 21, then the player is said to have blackjack.

The dealer **plays** the game along with the players. The dealer must **deal** the cards, **present** a player with additional cards, **show** all or part of a hand, **calculate** the value of all or part of a hand, calculate the number of cards in a hand, **determine** the winner, and **start** a new hand.

A card must **know** what its face value is and be able to **report** this value. The suit of the card is of no importance (but it might be for another game in the future). All cards must be members of a deck of cards. This deck must have the functionality to **deal** the next card, as well as **report** how many cards remain in the deck.

During the game, a player can **request** that a card be **dealt** to his or her hand. The player must be able to **display** the hand, **calculate** the face value of the hand, and **determine** the number of cards in the hand. When the dealer **asks** the player whether to deal another card or to **start** a new game, the player must **respond**.

Designing with Objects: The Software Development Process

CHAPTER 6

113

6

THE SOFTWARE
DEVELOPMENT
PROCESS

Each card has its own face value (suit does not factor into the face value). Aces count as 1 or 11. Face cards (Jack, Queen, King) each count as 10. The rest of the cards represent their face values.

The rules of the game state that if the sum of the face value of the player's cards is closer to 21 than the sum of the face value of the dealer's cards, the player **wins** an amount equal to the bet that was made. If the player **wins** with a blackjack, then the player **wins** 3:2 times the bet made (assuming that the dealer does not also have blackjack). If the sum of the face value of the player's cards exceeds 21, then the bet is **lost**. Blackjack (an ace and a face card or a 10) **beats** other combinations of 21.

If the player and the dealer have identical scores and at least 17, then it is considered a draw and the player **retains** the bet.

Now let's make a list of the possible responsibilities for our classes:

Card

- Know what its face value is.
- Know what its suit is.
- Know what its value is.
- Know if it is a face card.
- Know if it is an ace.
- Know if it is a joker.

Deck

- Shuffle.
- Deal the next card.
- Know how many cards are left in the deck.
- Know if there is a full deck to begin with.

Hand

- Know how many cards are in the hand.
- Know the value of the hand.

Dealer

- Deal the cards.
- Shuffle the deck.
- Give a card to a player.
- Show the dealer's hand.

- Calculate the value of the dealer's hand.
- Know the number of cards in the dealer's hand.
- Request a card (hit or hold).
- Determine the winner.
- Start a new hand.

Player

- Request a card (hit or hold).
- Show the player's hand.
- Calculate the value of the player's hand.
- Know how many cards are in the hand.
- Know whether the hand value is over 21.
- Know whether the hand value is equal 21 (and if it is a blackjack).
- Know whether the hand value is below 21.

Bet

- Know what type of bet it is.
- Know the value of the current bet.
- Know how much the player has left to bet.
- Know whether the bet can be covered.

Remember that this is just the initial pass. You will want to iterate through this a number of times and make changes. You might even find that you left an important responsibility out or that you need to split one responsibility into two responsibilities. Now let's explore each of the possible responsibilities:

We are left with the following classes and responsibilities:

Card

- Know what its face value is.

  The card definitely needs to know this. Internally, this class must track the value of the card. Because this is an implementation issue, we don't want to phrase the responsibility in this way. From an interface perspective, let's call this *display face value*.

- Know what its suit is.

  For the same reason as with face value, we will keep this responsibility, and rename it *display name* (which will identify the suit). However, we don't need this for blackjack. We will keep it for potential reuse purposes.

- ~~Know if it is a face card.~~

  We could have a separate responsibility for face cards, aces, and jokers, but the report value responsibility can probably handle this. Strike this responsibility.

- ~~Know if it is an ace.~~

  Same as above—let's strike this responsibility.

- ~~Know if it is a joker.~~

  Same as above, but notice that the joker was never mentioned in the requirements statement. This is a situation where we can add a responsibility to make the class more reusable. However, the responsibility for the joker goes to the report value, so let's strike this responsibility

---

WARNING

Warning

What to do with the jokers presents an interesting O-O design issue. Should there be two separate classes—a superclass representing a regular deck of cards (sans jokers) and a subclass representing a deck of cards with the addition of the jokers? From an O-O purist's perspective, having two classes may be the right approach. However, having a single class with two separate constructors may also be a valid approach. What happens if you have decks of cards that use other configurations (such as no aces or no Jacks)? Do we create a separate class for each or do we handle them in the main class?

This is another design issue that has no right or wrong answer.

Deck

- Shuffle.

  We definitely need to shuffle the deck, so let's keep this one.

- Deal the next card.

  We definitely need to deal the next card, so let's keep this one.

- Know how many cards are left in the deck.

  At least the dealer needs to know if there are any cards left, so let's keep this one.

- Know if there is a full deck to begin with.

  The deck must know if it includes all the cards. However, this may be strictly an internal implementation issue; in any event, let's keep this one for now.

Hand

- Know how many cards are in the hand.

    We definitely need to know how many cards are in a hand, so let's keep this one. However, from an interface perspective, let's rename this *report the number of cards in the hand.*

- Know the value of the hand.

    We definitely need to know the value of the hand, so let's keep this one. However, from an interface perspective, let's rename this *report the value of the hand.*

Dealer

- Deal the cards.

    The dealer must be able to deal the initial hand, so let's keep this one.

- Shuffle the deck.

    The dealer must be able to shuffle the deck, so let's keep this one. Actually, should we make the dealer request that the deck shuffle itself? Possibly.

- Give a card to a player.

    The dealer must be able to add a card to a player's hand, so let's keep this one.

- Show the dealer's hand.

    We definitely need this functionality, but this is a general function for all players, so perhaps the hand should show itself and the dealer should request this. Let's keep it for now.

- Calculate the value of the dealer's hand.

    Same as above. But the term *calculate* is an implementation issue in this case. Let's rename it *show the value of the dealer's hand.*

- Know the number of cards in the dealer's hand.

    Is this the same as *show the value of the dealer's hand*? Let's keep this for now but rename it *show the number of cards in the dealers hand.*

- Request a card (hit or hold).

    A dealer must be able to request a card. However, because the dealer is also a player, is there a way that we could share the code? While this is possible, for now we are going to treat a dealer and a player separately. Perhaps in another iteration through the design, we can use inheritance and factor out the commonality.

- Determine the winner.

    This depends on whether we want the dealer to calculate this or the game object. For now, let's keep it.

- Start a new hand.

    Same as above.

Player

- Request a card (hit or hold).

  A player must be able to request a card, so let's keep this one.

- Show the player's hand.

  We definitely need this functionality, but this is a general function for all players, so perhaps the hand should show itself and the dealer should request this. Let's keep this one for now.

- Calculate the value of the player's hand.

  Same as above. But the term *calculate* is an implementation issue in this case. Let's rename this *show the value of the player's hand.*

- Know how many cards are in the hand.

  Is this the same as *show the player's hand*? Let's keep this for now but rename it *show the number of cards in the player's hand.*

- Know whether the hand value is over 21, equal to 21 (including a blackjack), or below 21.

  Who should make this determination? These are based on the specific rules of the game. The player definitely needs to know this to make a decision about whether to request a card. In fact, the dealer needs to do this, too. This could be handled in *report the value of the hand.*

Bet

- Know what type of bet it is.

  At this point, we will keep this for future reuse; however, for this game we will require that the type of the bet is always money.

- Know the value of the current bet.

  We need this to keep track of the value of the current bet. The player and the dealer need to know this. We will assume that the dealer (that is, the house) has an unlimited amount to bet.

- Know how much the player has left to bet.

  In this case the bet can also act as the pool of money that the player has available. In this way, the player cannot make a bet that exceeds his or her resources.

- Know whether the bet can be covered.

  This is a simple response that allows the dealer (or the house) to determine whether the player can cover the bet.

As we iterate through the design process, we decide that we really do not want to have a separate bet class. If we need to, we can add it later. The decision needs to be based on two issues:

- Do we really need the class now or for future classes?
- Will it be easy to add later without a major redesign of the system?

After careful consideration, we decide that the class is not needed, and most probably will not be needed later. We make an assumption that the payment method for all future bets will be money. This is not necessarily a proper design decision. I can think of many reasons that we may want to have a bet object. There may be some behavior that should be encapsulated in a bet object. However, for now, we will scrap the bet object and make the dealer and players handle their own bets.

UML Use Cases: Identifying the Collaborations

To identify the collaborations, we need to study the responsibilities and determine what other classes the object interacts with. In short, what other classes does this object need to fulfill all its required responsibilities and complete its job? As you examine the collaborations, you might find that you have missed some necessary classes or that some classes that you initially identified are not needed:

- To help discover collaborations use-case scenarios can be used. A *use-case* is a transaction or sequence of related operations that the system performs in response to a user request or event.
- For each use-case, identify the objects and the messages that they exchange.
- You may want to create collaboration diagrams to document this step.

Obviously there can be an infinite number of scenarios. The purpose of this part of the process is not to document all possible scenarios, which is obviously an impossible task. The real purpose of creating use-case scenarios is to help you refine the choice of your classes and their responsibilities. By examining the collaborations, you might identify an important class that you missed. If this is the case, you can simply add another CRC card. You may also discover that one of the classes you originally chose is not as important as you once thought, so you can strike it and remove the CRC card from consideration. Whereas CRC cards help you discover classes, use-case scenarios help you discover collaborations.

For example, let's consider a single possible scenario. In this case we have a dealer and a single player.

- Dealer shuffles deck.
- Player makes bet.
- Dealer deals initial cards.

Designing with Objects: The Software Development Process

CHAPTER 6

119

6

THE SOFTWARE
DEVELOPMENT
PROCESS

- Player adds cards to player's hand.
- Dealer adds cards to dealer's hand.
- Hand returns value of player's hand to player.
- Hand returns value of dealer's hand to dealer.
- Dealer asks player if player wants another card.
- Dealer deals player another card.
- Player adds the card to player's hand.
- Hand returns value of player's hand to player.
- Dealer asks player if player wants another card.
- Dealer gets the value of the player's hand.
- Dealer sends or requests bet value from players.
- Player adds to/subtracts from player's bet attribute.

Let's determine some of the collaborations. Assume that we have a main application that contains all the objects (that is, we do not have a Game class). As part of our design we have the dealer start the game. Figures 6.6 through 6.15 present some collaboration diagrams pertaining to this initial design.

FIGURE 6.6
Start the game.

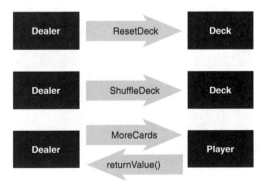

FIGURE 6.7
Shuffle and initially deal.

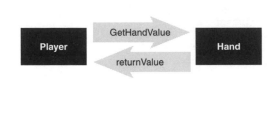

FIGURE 6.8
Get the hand value.

FIGURE 6.9
Get a card.

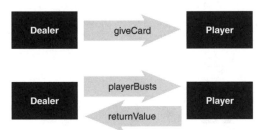

FIGURE 6.10
Deal a card and check to see if the player busts.

FIGURE 6.11
Return the value of the hand.

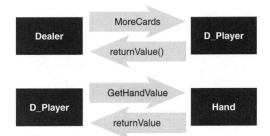

FIGURE 6.12
Does the dealer want more cards?

WARNING

Warning

Be aware that there are more issues than the value of a player's hand involved in deciding whether to take another card. A player at a real blackjack table might go with a gut feel or how the dealer's hand looks. While we might not be able to take gut feelings into consideration, we can attend to the issue of what the dealer's hand currently shows.

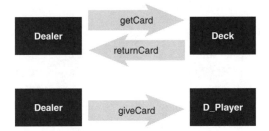

FIGURE 6.13
If requested, give the dealer a card.

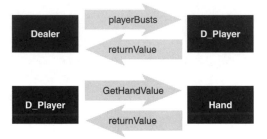

FIGURE 6.14
Does the dealer bust?

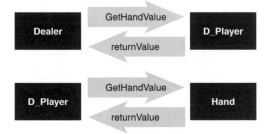

FIGURE 6.15
Do either the dealer or the player stand?

First Pass at CRC Cards

Now that we have identified the initial classes and the initial collaborations, we can complete the CRC cards for each class. It is important to note that these cards represent the initial pass only. In fact, while it is likely that many of the classes will survive the subsequent passes, the final list of classes and their corresponding collaborations may look nothing like what was gleaned from the initial pass. This exercise is meant to explain the process and create an initial pass, not to come up with a final design. Completing the design is a good exercise for you to undertake at the end of this chapter.

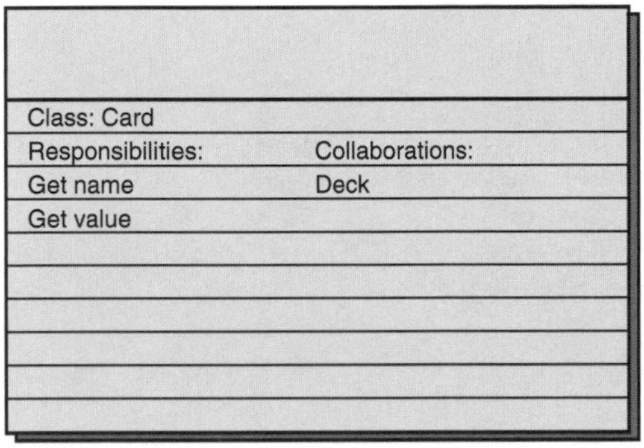

```
Class: Card
Responsibilities:        Collaborations:
Get name                 Deck
Get value
```

FIGURE 6.16
A CRC card for the Card *class.*

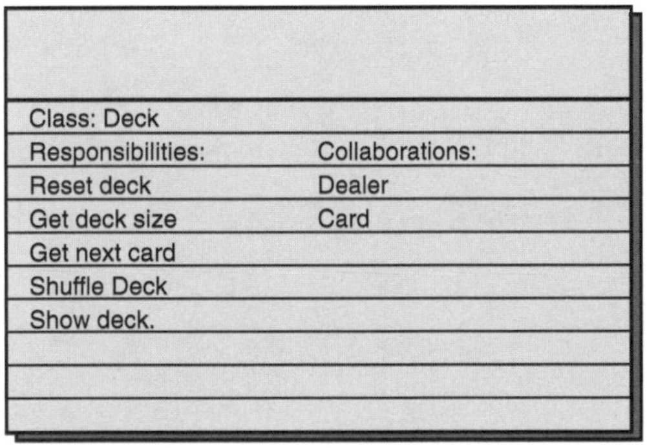

```
Class: Deck
Responsibilities:        Collaborations:
Reset deck               Dealer
Get deck size            Card
Get next card
Shuffle Deck
Show deck.
```

FIGURE 6.17
A CRC card for the Deck *class.*

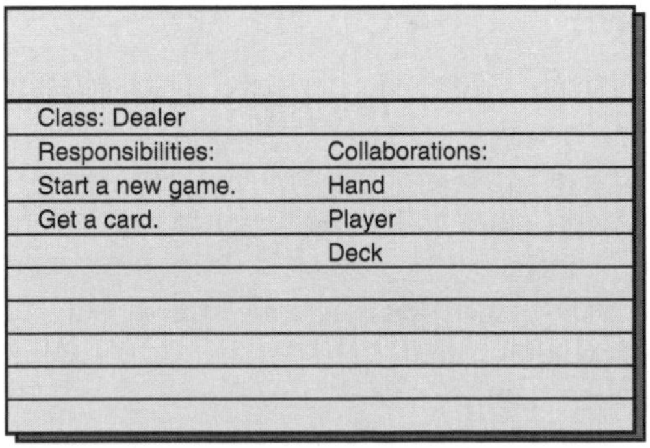

```
Class: Dealer
Responsibilities:        Collaborations:
Start a new game.        Hand
Get a card.              Player
                         Deck
```

FIGURE 6.18
A CRC card for the Dealer *class.*

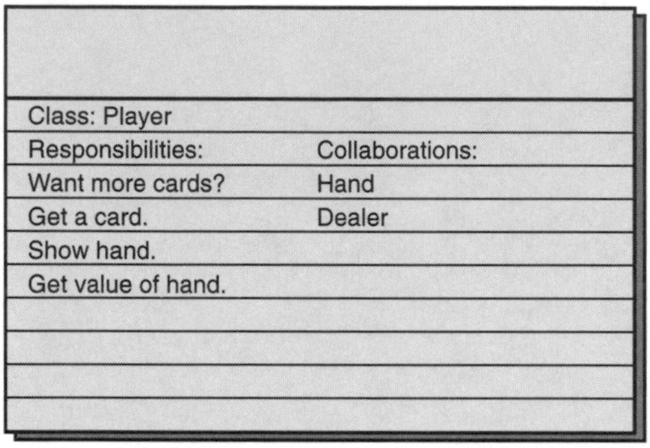

Class: Player	
Responsibilities:	Collaborations:
Want more cards?	Hand
Get a card.	Dealer
Show hand.	
Get value of hand.	

FIGURE 6.19
A CRC card for the Player class.

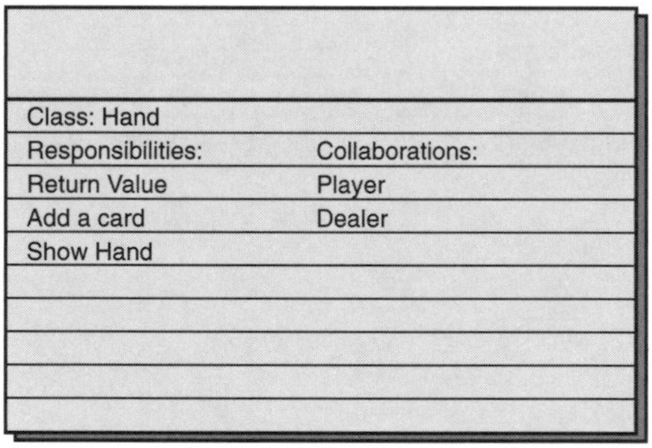

Class: Hand	
Responsibilities:	Collaborations:
Return Value	Player
Add a card	Dealer
Show Hand	

FIGURE 6.20
A CRC card for the Hand class.

UML Class Diagrams: The Object Model

After you have completed the initial design using CRC cards, transfer the information contained on the CRC cards to class diagrams (see Figure 6.21). Note that this class diagram represents one possible design – it does not represent the initial pass of classes created during the previous exercise. The class diagrams go beyond the information on the CRC cards and may include such information as, method parameters and return types. (Note that the UML diagrams in this book do not include method parameters.) Check out the options for the modeling tool that you have to see how information is presented. You can use the detailed form of the class diagram to document the implementation.

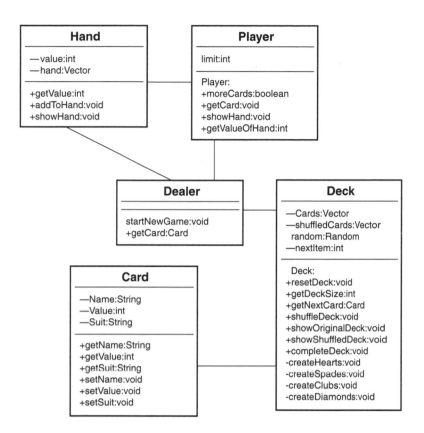

FIGURE 6.21

A UML diagram for the blackjack program.

Remember that the purpose of this exercise is to identify the classes and their interfaces. All the methods listed are public. Now a light bulb should be going off in your head.

Even though the search for the interfaces does not lead directly to private attributes and even private methods, the process is helpful in determining these as well. As you iterate through the CRC process, note what attributes and private methods each class will require.

Prototyping the User Interface

As our final step in the O-O design process, we must create a prototype of our user interface. This prototype will provide invaluable information to help navigate through the iterations of the design process. As Gilbert and McCarty, in their book *Object-Oriented Design in Java*, on page 180, aptly point out: *to a system user, the user interface is the system*. There are several ways to create a user interface prototype. You can sketch the user interface simply drawing it on paper or a white board. You can use a special prototyping tool, or even a language environment like Visual Basic which is often used for rapid prototyping. Or you can use the IDE from your favorite development tool to create the prototype.

However you develop the user interface prototype, make sure that the users have the final say on the look and feel.

Conclusion

This chapter covers the design process for complete systems. It focuses on combining several classes to build a system. This system is represented by UML class diagrams. The example in this chapter shows the first pass at creating a design and is not meant to be a finished design. Many iterations may be required to get the system model to the point were you are comfortable with it.

Implementing Some Blackjack Code

I recently came across a complete implementation of a blackjack game in the book *Java 1.1 Developers Guide* by Jamie Jaworski. If you would like to actually get your hands dirty and write some code to implement another blackjack design, you might want to pick up this book. It is a very good, compressive Java book.

In the next several chapters, we will explore in more detail the relationships between classes. Chapter 7, "Mastering Inheritance and Composition," covers the concepts of inheritance and composition and how they relate to each other.

References

Gilbert, Stephen, and Bill McCarty: *Object-Oriented Design in Java*. The Waite Group, 1998.

Jaworski, Jamie: *Java 1.1 Developers Guide*. Sams Publishing, 1997.

Wrifs-Brock, R., B. Wilkerson, and L. Weiner: *Designing Object-Oriented Software*. Prentice-Hall, 1990.

Ambler, Scott: *The Object Primer*. Cambridge University Press, 1998.

Weisfeld, Matt and John Ciccozzi: "Software by Committee," *Project Management Journal*, volume 5, number 1. Pages 30-36, September, 1999.

Mastering Inheritance and Composition

IN THIS CHAPTER

- Examine the finer points of inheritance
- Learn how to use composition in your design
- Determine when to use inheritance and when to use composition

Inheritance and composition play major roles in the design of object-oriented (O-O) systems. In fact, many of the most difficult, and interesting, design decisions come down to deciding between inheritance and composition.

Both inheritance and composition are mechanisms for reuse. *Inheritance*, as its name implies, involves inheriting attributes and behaviors from other classes. In this case, there is a true parent/child relationship. The child (or subclass) inherits directly from the parent (or superclass). Inheritance represents the is-a relationship that was introduced in Chapter 1, "Introduction to Object-Oriented Concepts." For example, a dog *is a* mammal.

Composition involves using other classes to build more complex classes. There is no parent/child relationship in this case. Basically, complex objects are composed of other objects. Composition represents a has-a relationship. For example, a car *has an* engine. Both the engine and the car are objects unto themselves. However, the car is a complex object that has an engine object. In fact, a child object may itself be composed of other objects; for example, the engine includes pistons.

TIP

A Real-World Example

It may be helpful in explaining the differences between is-a and has-a relationships based on terms from the relational database world. *Is-a* represents a hierarchical relationship between entity types (tables), whereas *has-a* represents a referential relationship.

When O-O technologies first entered the mainstream, inheritance was all the rage. The fact that you could design a class once and then inherit functionality from it was considered the foremost advantage to using O-O technologies. Reuse was the name of the game, and inheritance was the ultimate expression of reuse.

However, over the past few years the luster of inheritance has dulled a bit. In fact, if you listen to some people, inheritance should be avoided like the plague. It is interesting that the once shining star of O-O technologies has now become, in some circles, a sort of pariah. In their book *Java Design*, Peter Coad and Mark Mayfield have a complete chapter titled "Design with Composition Rather Than Inheritance." In fact, many object-based platforms do not even support true inheritance. Platforms such as the MS COM model, are based on interface inheritance. Interface inheritance is covered in great detail in Chapter 8, "Frameworks and Reuse: Designing with Interfaces and Abstract Classes."

The good news is that the discussions about whether to use inheritance or composition is a natural progression to some seasoned middle ground. As in all philosophical debates, there are fanatical people on both sides of the argument. Fortunately, as is normally the case, these heated discussions have led to a more sensible understanding of how to utilize the technologies.

For reasons that we will discuss later in this chapter, some people believe that inheritance should be avoided and composition should be the design method of choice. The argument is fairly complex and subtle. In actuality, both inheritance and composition are valid class design techniques and they each have their proper place in the O-O developer's toolkit.

The fact that inheritance is often misused and overused is more a result of a lack of understanding of what inheritance is all about than a fundamental flaw in using inheritance as a design strategy.

The bottom line is that inheritance and composition are both important techniques in building O-O systems. Designers and developers simply need to take the time to understand the strengths and weaknesses of both and to use each in the proper contexts.

Inheritance

Inheritance was defined in Chapter 1 as a system in which children inherit attributes and behavior from a parent class. However, there is more to inheritance, and in this chapter we will explore inheritance in greater detail.

Chapter 1 states that you can determine an inheritance relationship by following a simple rule: If Class B is a Class A, then this is a good candidate for inheritance.

TIP

Is-a

One of the primary rules of O-O design is that public inheritance is represented by an is-a relationship.

Let's revisit the mammal example used in Chapter 1. To present a very simple example, let's concentrate on a Dog class. A dog has several behaviors that make it distinctly a dog, as opposed to a cat. For this example let's specify two: A dog barks and a dog pants. So we can create a Dog class that has these two behaviors, along with two attributes (see Figure 7.1).

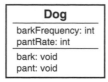

FIGURE 7.1

A class diagram for the Dog *class.*

Now, let's say that you want to create a GoldenRetriever class. You could create a brand new class that contains the same behaviors that the Dog class has. However, we can use the rule that we defined above: *A Golden Retriever is-a dog.* Because of this relationship, we can inherit the attributes and behavior from Dog and use it in our new GoldenRetriever class (see Figure 7.2).

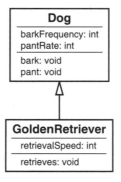

FIGURE 7.2

The GoldenRetriever *class inherits from the* Dog *class.*

The Golden Retriever class now contains its own behavior as well as all the more general behaviors of a dog. This provides us with some significant benefits. First, when we wrote the Golden Retriever class, we did not have to reinvent the wheel by writing the bark and pant methods over again. Not only does this save some coding time, but it saves testing time. The bark and pant methods are written only once and, assuming that they were properly tested when the Dog class was written, they do not need to be heavily tested again.

Now let's take full advantage of our inheritance structure and create a second class under the Dog class: a class called LhasaApso. Whereas a retriever is bred for retrieving, a LhasaApso is bred for use as guard dogs. These dogs are not attack dogs, they have acute senses, and when they sense something unusual, they start barking. So we can create our LhasaApso class and inherit from the Dog class just as we did with the GoldenRetriever class (see Figure 7.3).

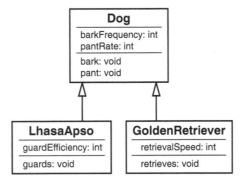

FIGURE 7.3

The LhasaApso class inherits from the Dog class.

TIP

Testing New Code

In our example with the GoldenRetriever class, the bark and pant methods should be written, tested, and debugged when the Dog class is written. Theoretically, this code is now robust and ready to reuse in other situations. However, the fact that you do not need to rewrite the code does not mean it should not be tested. Although it is unlikely, there may be some characteristic of a retriever that somehow breaks the code. The bottom line is that you should always test new code. Each new inheritance relationship creates a new context for using inherited methods. A complete testing strategy should take into account each of these contexts.

Another primary advantage of inheritance is that the code for bark() and pant() is in a single place. Let's say there is a need to change the code in the bark() method. When you change it in the bark() method, you do not need to change it in the LhasaApso class and the GoldenRetriever class.

Now, do you see a problem? This inheritance model appears to work great. However, can you be certain that that all dogs have the behavior contained in the Dog class?

In his book *Effective C++*, Scott Meyers gives a great example of a dilemma with design using inheritance. Consider a class for a bird. One of the most recognizable characteristics of a bird is that it can fly. So we create a class called Bird with a fly() method. Immediately you should understand the problem. What do we do with a penguin, or an ostrich? They are birds, but they can't fly. You could override the behavior locally, but the method would still be called `fly()`. And it would not make sense to have a method called `fly()` for a bird that does not fly, but only waddles.

In our dog example, we have designed in the fact that all dogs can bark. However, there are dogs that do not bark. A breed called `Basenji` is a barkless dog: These dogs do not bark, but they yodel. So should we reevaluate our design? What would this design look like? Figure 7.4 is an example that shows a more correct way to model the hierarchy of the `Dog` class.

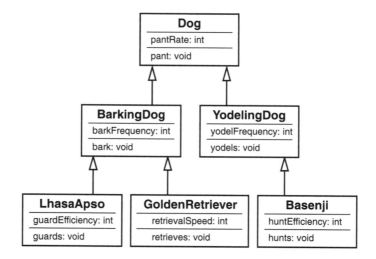

FIGURE 7.4
The Dog *class hierarchy.*

Generalization and Specialization

Consider the object model of the `Dog` class hierarchy. We started with a single class, called `Dog`, and we factored out some of the commonality between various breeds of dogs. This concept, sometimes called *generalization-specialization*, is yet another important consideration when using inheritance. The idea is that as you make your way down the inheritance tree, things get more specific. The most general case is at the top of the tree. In our `Dog` inheritance tree, the class `Dog` is at the top and is the most general category. The various breeds—the `GoldenRetriever`, `LhasaApso`, and `Basenji` classes—are the most specific. The idea of inheritance is to go from the general to the specific by factoring out commonality.

In the `Dog` inheritance model, we started factoring out common behavior by understanding that although a retriever has some different behavior from that of a `LhasaApso`, the breeds do share some common behaviors—for example, they both pant and bark. Then we realized that all dogs do not bark, some yodel. Thus, we had to factor out the barking behavior into a separate `BarkingDog` class. The yodeling behavior went into a `YodelingDog` class. However, we still realized that both barking dogs and barkless dogs still shared some common behavior—that all dogs pant. Thus, we kept the `Dog` class and had the `BarkingDog` and the `YodelingDog` classes inherit from `Dog`. Now `Basenji` can inherit from `YodelingDog`, and `LhasaApso` and `GoldenRetriever` can inherit from `BarkingDog`.

It's All in the Design

In theory, factoring out as much commonality as possible is great. However, as in all design issues, sometimes it really is too much of a good thing. Although factoring out as much commonality as possible may well represent real-life as closely as possible, it may not represent your model as closely as possible. The more you factor out, the more complex your system gets. So you have a conundrum: Do you want to live with a more accurate model or a system with less complexity? You have to make this choice based on your situation, for there are no hard guidelines to make the decision.

> **WARNING**
>
> Obviously a computer model can only approximate real-world situations. Computers are good at number crunching, but are not as good at more abstract operations.

For example, breaking up the `Dog` class into `BarkingDog` and the `YodelingDog` models real life better than assuming that all dogs bark but it does add a bit of complexity.

> **TIP**
>
> ### Model Complexity
>
> At this level of our example, adding two more classes does not make things so complex that it makes the model untenable. However, in larger systems, when these kinds of decisions are made over and over, the complexity quickly adds up. In larger systems, keeping things as simple as possible is usually the best practice.

There will be instances in your design when the advantage of a more accurate model does not warrant the additional complexity. Let's assume that you are a dog breeder and that you contract out for a system that tracks all your dogs. The system model that includes barking dogs and yodeling dogs works fine. However, suppose that you simply do not breed any yodeling dogs—never have and never will. Perhaps you do not need to include the complexity of differentiating between yodeling dogs and barking dogs. This will make your system less complex and it will provide the functionality that you need.

Deciding whether or not to design for less complexity or more functionality is really a balancing act. The primary goal is always to build a system that is flexible without adding so much complexity that the system collapses under its own weight. Current and future costs are also a major factor in these decisions. Although it might seem appropriate to make a system more complete and flexible, this added functionality might barely add any benefit. In short, the return on investment is just not there. For example, would you extend the design of your Dog system to include other canines, such as hyenas and foxes (see Figure 7.5)?

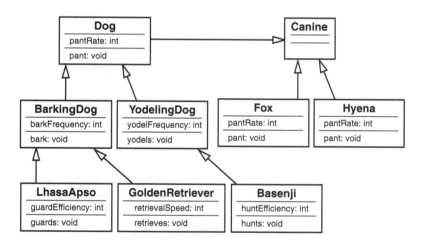

FIGURE 7.5
An expanded canine model.

Now, although this design might be prudent if you were a zookeeper, the extension of the Canine class is probably not necessary if you are breeding and selling domesticated dogs.

So as you can see, there are always tradeoffs when creating a design.

> **TIP**
>
> ## Making Design Decisions with the Future in Mind
>
> You may at this point say "never say never." Although you might not breed yodeling dogs now, sometime in the future you might want to do so. If you do not design for the possibility of yodeling dogs now, it will be much more expensive to change the system later to include them. This is yet another design decision that you have to make. You could possibly override the bark() method to make it yodel; however, this is not intuitive as some people will expect a method called bark() to actually bark.

Composition

It is natural to think of objects as containing other objects. A television set contains a tuner and video display. A computer contains video cards, keyboards, and floppy drives. The computer can be considered an object unto itself, and the floppy drive is also considered a valid object. You could open up the computer and remove the floppy drive and hold it in your hand. In fact, you could take the floppy drive to another computer and install it; because it works in multiple computers, the fact that it is a standalone object is reinforced.

The classic example of object composition is the automobile. Many books, training classes, and articles seem to use the automobile as the essence of object composition. Besides the original interchangeable manufacture of the rifle, most people think of the automobile assembly line created by Henry Ford as the quintessential example of interchangeable parts. Thus, it seems natural that the automobile has become a primary reference point for designing O-O software systems.

For example, most people would think it natural for a car to contain an engine. In fact, a car contains many objects besides an engine, including wheels, a steering wheel, and a stereo. Whenever a particular object is composed of other objects, and those objects are included as object fields, the new object is known as a compound, an aggregate, or a composite object (see Figure 7.6).

> **TIP**
>
> ## Aggregation and Composition
>
> Sometimes a distinction is made between the words *aggregation* and *composition*. However, in this book we will consider composition and aggregation as the same thing.

A Car has a Steering Wheel

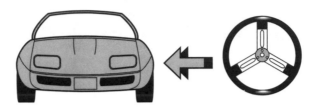

FIGURE 7.6
An example of composition.

Representing Composition with UML

To represent the fact that the car object contains a steering wheel object, UML uses the notation shown in Figure 7.7.

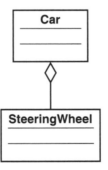

FIGURE 7.7
Representing composition in the UML.

Note that the line connecting the Car class to the SteeringWheel class has a diamond shape on the Car side of the line. This signifies that a Car *contains* (has-a) SteeringWheel.

Let's expand this example. Let's say that none of the objects used in this design use inheritance in any way. All the object relationships are strictly composition, and there are multiple levels of composition. Of course, this is a simplistic example and there are many, many more object and object relationships in designing a car. However, this design is simply meant to be a simple illustration of what composition is all about.

Let's say that a car is composed of an engine, a stereo system, and a door.

TIP

How Many Doors and Stereos?

Note that a car normally has more than one door. Some have two, and some have four. You may even consider a hatchback a fifth door. In the same vein, it is not necessarily true that all cars have a stereo system. A car could have no stereo system or it could have one. I have even seen a car with two separate stereo systems. These situations are discussed in detail in Chapter 9, "Building Objects." For now, for the sake of this example, just pretend that a car has only a single door (perhaps a special racing car) and a single stereo system.

The fact that a car is made up of an engine, a stereo system, and a door is easy to understand because most people think of cars in this way. However, it is important to keep in mind when designing software systems, just like automobiles, that objects are made up of other objects. In fact, the number of nodes and branches that can be included in this tree structure of classes is virtually unlimited.

Figure 7.8 shows the object model for the car, with the engine, stereo system, and door included.

Note that all three objects that make up a car are themselves composed of other objects. The engine contains pistons and spark plugs. The stereo contains a radio and a cassette. The door contains a handle. Also note that there is yet another level. The radio contains a tuner. We could have also added the fact that a handle contains a lock, the cassette contains a fast forward button, and so on. Additionally, we could have gone one level beyond the tuner and created an object for a dial. The level and complexity of the object model is, obviously, up to the designer.

TIP

Model Complexity

As with the inheritance problem of the barking and yodeling dogs, using too much composition can also lead to more complexity. There is a fine line between creating an object model that contains enough granularity to be sufficiently expressive and a model that is so granular that it is difficult to understand and maintain.

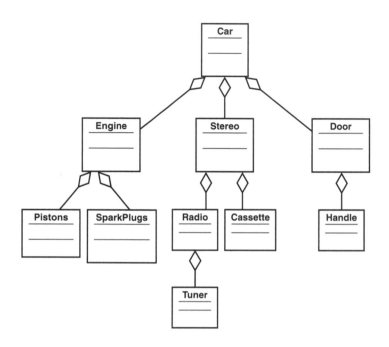

FIGURE 7.8
The Car *class hierarchy.*

Why Encapsulation Is Fundamental to O-O

Encapsulation is really the fundamental concept of O-O. Whenever the interface/implementation paradigm is covered, we are really talking about encapsulation. The basic question is what in a class should be exposed and what should not be exposed. This encapsulation pertains equally to data and behavior. When talking about a class, the primary design decision revolves around encapsulating both the data and the behavior into a well-written class.

In the book *Object-Oriented Design in Java*, Stephen Gilbert and Bill McCarty define encapsulation as "the process of packaging your program, dividing each of its classes into two distinct parts: the interface and the implementation." This is the message that has been presented over and over again in this book.

But what does encapsulation have to do with inheritance, and how does it apply with regard to this chapter? This has to do with an O-O paradox. Encapsulation is so fundamental to O-O that it is one of O-O design's cardinal rules. Inheritance is also considered one of the three primary O-O concepts. However, in one way, inheritance actually breaks encapsulation! How can this be? Is it possible that two of the three primary concepts of O-O are incompatible with each other? Well, let's explore this possibility.

How Inheritance Weakens Encapsulation

As already stated, encapsulation is the process of packaging classes into the public interface and the private implementation. In essence, a class hides everything that is not necessary for other classes to know about.

In the book *Java Design*, Second Edition, Peter Coad and Mark Mayfield make a case that when using inheritance, encapsulation is inherently weakened within a class hierarchy. They talk about a specific risk: Inheritance connotes strong encapsulation with other classes, but weak encapsulation between a superclass and its subclasses.

The problem is that if you inherit an implementation from a superclass, and then change that implementation, the change *ripples through* the class hierarchy. This rippling effect potentially affects all the subclasses. At first, this may not seem like a major problem; however, as we have seen, a rippling effect such as this can cause unanticipated problems. For example, testing can become a nightmare. In Chapter 6, "Designing with Objects: The Software Design Process," we talked about the fact that encapsulation makes testing systems easier. In theory, if you create a class called `Cabbie` (see Figure 7.9) with the appropriate public interfaces, any change to the implementation of `Cabbie` should be transparent to all other classes. If the other classes were directly dependent on the implementation of the `Cabbie` class, then testing would become more difficult, if not untenable.

7

MASTERING
INHERITANCE AND
COMPOSITON

> **TIP**
>
> ## Keep Testing
> Even with encapsulation, you would still want to retest the classes that use `Cabbie` to verify that no problem has, in fact, been introduced by the change.

If you then subclass `Cabbie` with a class called `PartTimeCabbie`, and `PartTimeCabbie` inherits the implementation from `Cabbie`, changing the implementation of `Cabbie` directly affects the `PartTimeCabbie` class.

For example, consider the UML diagram in Figure 7.10. `PartTimeCabbie` is a subclass of `Cabbie`. Thus, `PartTimeCabbie` inherits the public implementation of `Cabbie`, including the method `giveDirections()`. If the method `giveDirections` is changed in `Cabbie`, it will have a direct impact on `PartTimeCabbie` and any other classes that may later be subclasses of `Cabbie`. In this subtle way, changes to the implementation of `Cabbie` are not necessarily encapsulated within the `Cabbie` class.

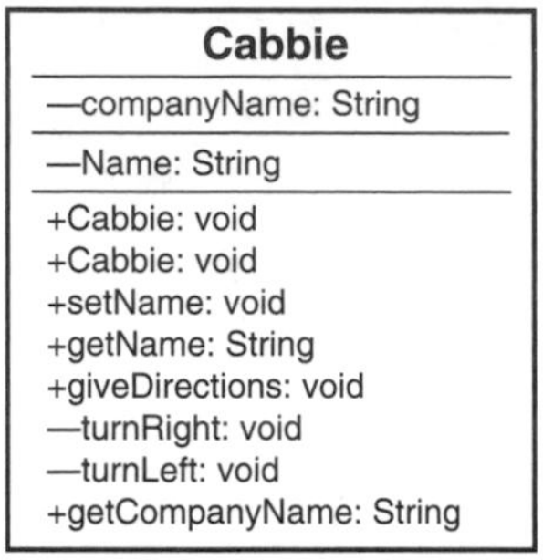

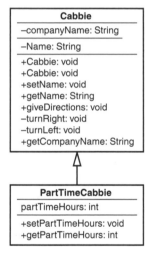

FIGURE 7.9
A UML Diagram of the Cabbie *Class.*

FIGURE 7.10
A UML Diagram of the Cabbie/PartTimeCabbie *Classes.*

To reduce the risk posed by this dilemma, it is important that you stick to the strict is-a condition when using inheritance. If the subclass is truly a specialization of the superclass, then changes to the parent would likely affect the child in ways that are natural and expected. To illustrate, if a Circle class inherits implementation from a Shape class, and a change to the implementation of Shape breaks Circle, then Circle was not truly a Shape to begin with.

How can inheritance be used improperly? Consider a situation in which you want to create a window for the purposes of a graphical user interface (GUI). One impulse may be to create a window by making it a subclass of a rectangle class:

```
class Rectangle {

}

class Window extends Rectangle {

}
```

In reality a GUI window is much, much more than a rectangle. It is not really a specialized version of a rectangle, as is a square. A true window may contain a rectangle (in fact many rectangles); however, it is really not a true rectangle. In this approach, a `Window` class should not *inherit* from `Rectangle`, but it should *contain* `Rectangle` classes:

```
class Window {

    Rectangle menubar;
    Rectangle statusbar;
    Rectangle mainview;

}
```

A Detailed Example of Polymorphism

Many people consider polymorphism the cornerstone of O-O design. Designing a class for the purpose of creating totally independent objects is what O-O is all about. In a well-designed system, an object should be able to answer all the important questions about itself. As a rule, an object should be responsible for itself. This independence is one of the primary mechanisms of code reuse.

As stated in Chapter 1, *polymorphism* literally means many shapes. When a message is sent to an object, the object must have a method defined to respond to that message. In an inheritance hierarchy, all subclasses inherit the interfaces from their superclass. However, because each subclass is a separate entity, each might require a separate response to the same message.

To review the example in Chapter 1, consider a class called `Shape`. This class has a behavior called `Draw`. However, when you tell somebody to draw a shape, the first question they ask is likely to be, "What shape?" Simply telling a person to draw a shape is too abstract (in fact, the `Draw` method in `Shape` contains no implementation). You must specify which shape you mean. To do this, you provide the actual implementation in `Circle` and other subclasses. Even though `Shape` has a `Draw` method, `Circle` *overrides* this method and provides its own `Draw` method. Overriding basically means replacing an implementation of a parent with your own.

An Object Should Be Responsible for Itself

Let's revisit the Shape example from Chapter 1 (see Figure 7.11).

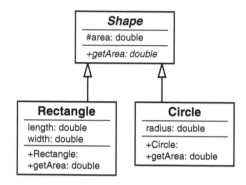

FIGURE 7.11

The Shape *class hierarchy.*

Polymorphism is one of the most elegant uses of inheritance. Remember that a Shape cannot be instantiated. It is an abstract class. Chapter 8 explains abstract classes in great detail.

However, Rectangle and Circle can be instantiated because they are concrete classes. Rectangle and Circle are both shapes; however, they obviously have some differences. Because Rectangle and Circle are both shapes, their area can be calculated. Yet, the formula to calculate the area is different for each. Thus, the area formulas cannot be placed in the Shape class.

This is where polymorphism comes in. The premise of polymorphism is that you can send messages to various objects, and they will respond according to their object type. For example, if you send the message getArea() to a Circle class, you will invoke a completely different method than if you send the same getArea message to a Rectangle class. This is because both Circle and Rectangle are responsible for themselves. If you ask Circle to return its area, it knows how to do this. If you want a circle to draw itself, it can do this, too. A Shape object could not do this even if it could be instantiated. Notice that in the UML diagram the getArea() method in the Shape class is italicized. This designates that the method is abstract.

As a very simple example, imagine that there are four classes: the abstract class Shape, and concrete classes Circle, Rectangle, and Star. Here is the code:

```
public abstract class Shape{

    public abstract void draw();

}
```

```
public class Circle extends Shape{

    public void draw() {

        System.out.println("I am drawing a Circle");

    };
}

public class Rectangle extends Shape{

    public void draw() {

        System.out.println("I am drawing a Rectangle");

    };
}

public class Star extends Shape{

    public void draw() {

        System.out.println("I am drawing a Star");

    };
}
```

Notice that there is only one method for each class: draw(). Here is the important point regarding polymorphism and an object being responsible for itself: The concrete classes themselves have responsibility for the drawing function. The Shape class does not provide the code for drawing; the Circle, Rectangle, and Star classes do this for themselves. Here is some code to prove it:

```
public class TestShape {

    public static void main(String args[]) {

        Circle circle = new Circle();
        Rectangle rectangle = new Rectangle();
        Star star = new Star();

        circle.draw();
        rectangle.draw();
        star.draw();

    }

}
```

TIP

Compiling This Code

If you want to compile this Java code, make sure that you set `classpath` to the current directory:

```
javac -classpath . Shape.java
javac -classpath . Circle.java
javac -classpath . Rectangle.java
javac -classpath . Star.java
javac -classpath . TestShape.java
```

Actually, when you compile a Java class (in this case `TestShape`), and it requires another class (let's say `Circle`) the javac compiler will attempt to compile all the required classes. Thus, the following line will actually compile all the files in this example.

```
javac -classpath . TestShape.java
```

The test application `TestShape` creates three classes: `Circle`, `Rectangle`, and `Star`. To actually draw these classes, `TestShape` simply asks the individual classes to draw themselves:

```
circle.draw();
rectangle.draw();
star.draw();
```

When you execute `TestShape`, you get the following results:

```
C:\>java TestShape
I am drawing a Circle
I am drawing a Rectangle
I am drawing a Star
```

This is polymorphism at work. What would happen if you wanted to create a new shape, say `Triangle`? Simply write the class, compile it, test it, and use it. The base class `Shape` does not have to change—nor does any other code:

```
public class Triangle extends Shape{

    public void draw() {

        System.out.println("I am drawing a Triangle");

    };
}
```

A message can now be sent to `Triangle`. And even though `Shape` does not know how to draw a triangle, the `Triangle` class does:

```java
public class TestShape {

    public static void main(String args[]) {

        Circle circle = new Circle();
        Rectangle rectangle = new Rectangle();
        Star star = new Star();
        Triangle triangle = new Triangle ();

        circle.draw();
        rectangle.draw();
        star.draw();
        triangle.draw();

    }

}
```

```
C:\>java TestShape
I am drawing a Circle
I am drawing a Rectangle
I am drawing a Star
I am drawing a Triangle
```

To see the real power of polymorphism, you can actually pass the shape to a method that has absolutely no idea what shape is coming.

```java
public class TestShape {

    public static void main(String args[]) {

        Circle circle = new Circle();
        Rectangle rectangle = new Rectangle();
        Star star = new Star();

        drawMe(circle);
        drawMe(rectangle);
        drawMe(star);

    }

    static void drawMe(Shape s) {
        s.draw();
    }

}
```

In this case, the Shape object can be passed to the method drawMe() and the drawMe() method can handle any valid Shape—even one you add later. You can run this version of TestShape just like the previous one.

Conclusion

This chapter gives a basic overview of what inheritance and composition are and how they are different. Many well-respected O-O designers have stated that composition should be used whenever possible, and inheritance should be used only when necessary.

However, as stated in the introduction to this chapter, this is a bit simplistic. I believe that the idea that composition should be used whenever possible hides the real issue. The real issue may simply be that composition is more appropriate in more cases than inheritance—not that it should be used whenever possible. The fact that composition may be more appropriate in most cases does not mean that inheritance is evil. Use both composition and inheritance, but only in their proper contexts.

In earlier chapters the concepts of abstract classes and Java interfaces arose several times. In Chapter 8, we will explore the concept of development contracts and how abstract classes and Java interfaces are used to satisfy these contracts.

References

Coad, Peter, and Mark Mayfield: *Java Design*. Object International, 1999.

Meyers, Scott: *Effective C++*. Addison-Wesley, 1992.

Gilbert, Stephen, and Bill McCarty: *Object-Oriented Design in Java*. The Waite Group, 1998.

Frameworks and Reuse: Designing with Interfaces and Abstract Classes

IN THIS CHAPTER

- Understand the concept of a framework

- Learn what a programming contract is

- Delve deeper into the concept of an abstract class

- Learn the difference between an abstract class and a Java interface

Chapter 7, "Mastering Inheritance and Composition," explains how inheritance and composition play major roles in the design of object-oriented (O-O) systems. This chapter expands on this theme and introduces the concepts of a Java interface and an abstract class.

Java interfaces and abstract classes are a powerful mechanism for code reuse, providing the foundation for a concept we will call *contracts*. This chapter covers the topics of code reuse, frameworks, contracts, Java interfaces, and abstract classes. At the end of the chapter, we'll work through an example of how all these concepts can be applied to a real-world situation.

To Reuse or Not to Reuse?

You have probably heard people singing the praises of code reuse since you took your first computer class or wrote your first line of code. Some people consider code reuse to be the savior of the software development community. Since the dawn of computer software, the concept of reusing code has been reinvented several times. The O-O paradigm is no different. One of the major advantages touted by O-O proponents is that you can write code once, and then reuse it to your heart's content.

This is true to a certain degree. As with all design approaches, the utility and the reusability of code depend on how well it was designed and implemented. O-O design does not hold the patent on code reuse. There is nothing stopping anyone from writing very robust and reusable code in a non–O-O language. Certainly, there are countless numbers of routines and functions, written in structured languages such as COBOL and C, that are of high quality and quite reusable.

Thus, it is clear that following the O-O paradigm is not the only way to develop reusable code. Yet the O-O approach does provide several mechanisms for facilitating the development of reusable code. One way to create reusable code is to create frameworks. In this chapter we focus on using interfaces and abstract classes to create frameworks and encourage reusable code.

What Is a Framework?

Hand-in-hand with the concept of code reuse is the concept of *standardization*, which is sometimes called *plug-and-play*. The idea of a framework revolves around these plug-and-play and reuse principles. One of the classic examples of a framework is a desktop application. Let's take an office suite application as an example. The document editor that I am currently using (Microsoft Word) has a menu bar that includes multiple menu options. These options are similar to those in the presentation package (Microsoft PowerPoint) and the spreadsheet software (Microsoft Excel) that I also have open. In fact, the first six menu items (File, Edit, View, Insert, Format, and Tools) are the same in all three programs. Not only are the menu options similar, but the first toolbar looks remarkably alike as well (New, Open, Save, and so on). Below the toolbars is the document area—whether it be for a document, a presentation, or a spreadsheet. The common framework makes it easier to learn various applications within the office suite. It also makes a developer's life easier by allowing maximum code reuse.

The fact that all these menu bars have a similar look and feel is obviously not an accident. In fact, when you develop in most integrated development environments, on a certain platform like Microsoft Windows, for example, you get certain things without having to create them yourself. When you create a window in a Windows environment, you get elements like the main title bar and the file close button in the top-right corner. When you double-click on the main title bar, the screen always minimizes/maximizes. When you click on the close button in the top-right corner, the application always terminates. This is all part of the framework. Figure 8.1 is a screen shot of a word processor. Note the menu bars, toolbars, and other elements that are part of the framework.

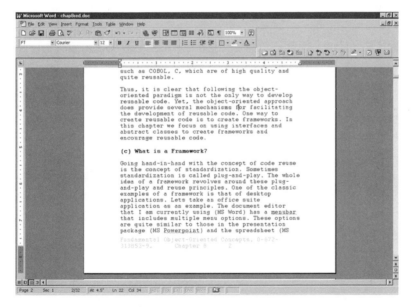

FIGURE 8.1

A word processing framework.

A word processing framework generally includes operations such as creating documents; opening documents; saving documents; cutting, copying, and pasting text; searching through documents; and so on. To use this framework, a developer must use a predetermined interface to create an application. This pre-determined interface conforms to the standard framework, which has two obvious advantages. First, as we have already seen, the look and feel are consistent, and the end users do not have to learn a new framework. Second, a developer can take advantage of code that has already been written and tested (and this testing issue should not be underestimated). Why write code to create a brand new Open dialog when one already exists and has been thoroughly tested? In a business setting, when time is critical, people do not want to have to learn new things unless it is absolutely necessary.

> ### TIP
>
> ### Code Reuse Revisited
> In Chapter 7, we talked about code reuse as it pertains to inheritance—basically one class inheriting from another class. This chapter is about frameworks and reusing whole or partial systems.

You might next wonder how you use the dialog box provided by the framework. The answer is simple: You follow the rules that the framework provides you. And where might you find these rules? The rules for the framework are found in the documentation. The person or persons who wrote the class, classes, or class libraries should have provided documentation on how to use the public interfaces of the class, classes, or class libraries (at least we hope). In many cases this takes the form of the application programming interface (API).

For example, to create an applet in Java, you would bring up the API documentation for the Applet class and take a look at the public interfaces it presents. Figure 8.2 shows a part of the Java API. By using these APIs, you can create a valid Java applet and conform to required standards. If you follow these standards, your applet will be set to run in Java-enabled browsers.

What Is a Contract?

In the context of this book, we will consider a *contract* to be any mechanism that requires a developer to comply with the specifications of an API framework. The online dictionary Dictionary.com (www.dictionary.com) defines a contact as "an agreement between two or more parties, especially one that is written and enforceable by law."

This is exactly what happens when a developer uses an API—with the project manager or business owner representing the law. When a developer agrees to follow a framework, the developer is, in effect, making a contract with the provider of the framework. As is always the case, the contract must be enforceable. Thus, the project manager, or business owner, must ensure that everyone involved with the project conforms to the contract.

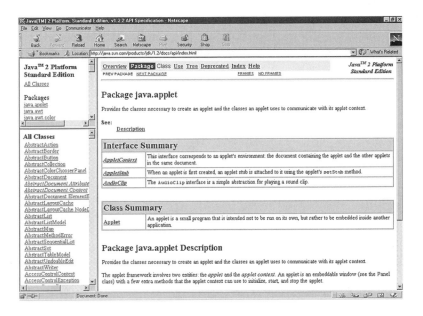

FIGURE 8.2

API documentation.

Enforcement is vital because it is possible for a developer to break a contract. Without enforcement a rogue developer could decide to reinvent the wheel and write his or her own code rather than use the code provided by the framework. There is little benefit to a standard if people routinely disregard it.

In Java, the two ways to implement contracts are to use abstract classes and interfaces. Before we go any further, let's explore both of these concepts.

Abstract Classes

One way a contract is implemented is via an abstract class. An *abstract class* is a class that contains one or more methods that do not have any implementation provided. This goes back to the section "Polymorphism" in Chapter 1, "Introduction to Object-Oriented Concepts," where we discussed the concept of abstract versus concrete classes. Suppose that you have an abstract class called Shape. The reason it is considered abstract is because you cannot instantiate it. If you ask someone to draw a shape, the first thing they will probably ask you is "What kind of shape?" Thus, the idea of a shape is abstract. However, if someone asks you to draw a circle, this does not pose a problem because a circle is a concrete concept. You know how to draw a circle. You also know how to draw other shapes, such as a rectangle.

How does this apply to a class? At the abstract level, we know that we can draw a shape. In fact, we want to be able to draw every kind of shape represented in our system, even ones that will be added later. We also want them all to use the same syntax when drawing—let's say a method called Draw. Thus, we want to ensure that every shape implemented in our system has a Draw method that can draw itself. When we ultimately create classes called Circle and Rectangle, which are subclasses of Shape, these classes must implement their own version of Draw (see Figure 8.3).

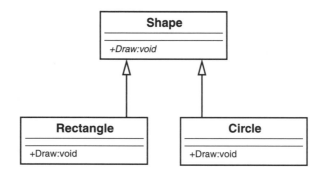

FIGURE 8.3
An Abstract Class Hierarchy.

In this way, we have a Shape framework that is truly polymorphic. The Draw method can be invoked for every shape in the system, and invoking each shape produces a different result. Invoking the Draw method on a Circle object draws a circle, and invoking the Draw method on a Rectangle object draws a rectangle. In essence, sending a message to an object evokes a different response, depending on the object. This is the essence of polymorphism.

Let's look at some code to illustrate how Rectangle and Circle conform to the contract that Shape offered, by implementing the Draw method. Here is the code for the Shape class:

```
public abstract class Shape {

    public abstract void Draw();

}
```

Note that the class does not provide any implementation for Draw. There are two reasons for this. First, Shape does not know what to draw, so we could not implement the Draw method even if we wanted to. Second, we want the subclasses to provide the implementation. Let's look at the Circle and Rectangle classes:

```
public class Circle extends Shape {

    public void Draw() {System.out.println ("Draw a Circle"};

}

public class Rectangle extends Shape {

    public void Draw() {System.out.println ("Draw a Rectangle"};

}
```

Note that both `Circle` and `Rectangle` extend (that is, inherit from) `Shape`. Also notice that they provide the actual implementation (in this case the implementation is obviously trivial). If, for example, `Circle` did not provide an implementation for `Draw`, then it would fail in its attempt to satisfy the contract with `Shape`, and it would itself become an abstract class. In this case, some other class would have to be a subclass of `Circle` and provide an implementation of `Draw`. This subclass would then become the concrete implementation of both `Shape` and `Circle`.

WARNING

Be aware that in the cases of `Shape`, `Circle`, and `Rectangle`, we are dealing with a strict inheritance relationship, as opposed to an interface, which we will discuss in the next section. `Circle` is a `Shape` and `Rectangle` is a `Shape`. This is an important point because contracts are not meant to be used in cases of composition or has-a relationships.

Although the concept of abstract classes revolves around abstract methods, there is nothing stopping `Shape` from actually providing some implementation. For example, although `Circle` and `Rectangle` implement the `Draw` method differently, they share the same mechanism for setting the color of the shape. So the `Shape` class can have a color attribute and a method to set the color. This `setColor` method is an actual implementation and would be inherited by `Circle` and `Rectangle`. The only methods that a subclass must implement are the ones that the superclass declares as abstract. These abstract methods are the contract.

Some languages, such as C++, use only abstract classes to implement contracts. Java, however, has another mechanism to implement a contract: an interface.

Interfaces

Now it is time to alleviate some possible confusion. You have heard the term *interface* bounced around since Chapter 1. In earlier chapters, when interfaces were discussed, they were mentioned in the context of public entry points (that is, methods) to a class. In this chapter, we introduce the concept of a Java language context called an *interface*.

WARNING

The term *interface* used in earlier chapters is a term generic to O-O programming and refers to the public interface to a class. The term *Java interface* refers to a language construct that is specific to Java. It is important not to get the two terms confused. (Actually, interfaces are not specific to only Java; other O-O languages use them as well.)

Although the Java interface is obviously specific to the Java language, we discuss it here because of Java's popularity and the importance of the interface to the design of Java systems. For languages such as C++, using an abstract class provides the same functionality, even if perhaps not quite as eloquently.

If an abstract class can provide the same functionality as an interface, why does Java have an interface? For one thing, as we already know, Java does not allow multiple inheritance. At a certain level, Java interfaces are a way to implement some degree of multiple inheritance. Although a Java class can inherit from only one class, it can implement many interfaces. Thus, although Java does not support strict multiple inheritance, it does support multiple interfaces. However, saying that Java interfaces are a way to circumvent the lack of multiple inheritance is short-changing the true power of the interface. Interfaces are a powerful way to enforce contracts for a framework. Let's talk more about interfaces.

TIP

Implementation Versus Definition Inheritance

Sometimes inheritance is referred to as *implementation inheritance* and interfaces are called *definition inheritance*.

First, let's consider an interface called `Nameable`, as shown in Figure 8.4.

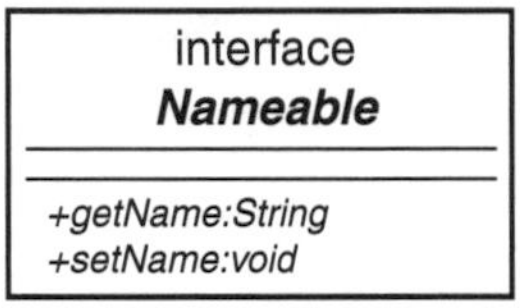

```
             ┌─────────────────────────┐
             │       interface         │
             │       *Nameable*        │
             ├─────────────────────────┤
             │ +getName:String         │
             │ +setName:void           │
             └─────────────────────────┘
```

FIGURE 8.4

A UML diagram of a Java interface.

Note that Nameable is identified in the UML diagram as an interface. Also note that there are two methods, getName and setName. Here is the corresponding code:

```java
public interface Nameable {

    String getName();
    void setName (String aName);

}
```

In the code, notice that Nameable is not declared as a class, but as an interface. Because of this, both methods, getName and setName, are considered abstract and there is no implementation provided. An interface, unlike an abstract class, can provide no implementation. As a result, any class that implements an interface must provide the implementation (that is, the executable code).

Interfaces are meant to specify behavior. In the case of the Nameable interface, our intent is to indicate that something is nameable. We can make conventions to help in this matter. There are several conventions for naming interfaces. In this book, we always end an interface with the suffix able (another common convention is to put a capital I in front of the name—such as INameable). Here we call the interface Nameable. This can be confusing, so let's discuss the differences between an abstract class and a Java interface in more detail.

Assume that we want to design a class that represents a dog, with the intent of adding more mammals later. The logical move would be to create an abstract class called Mammal:

```java
public abstract class Mammal {

    public void generateHeat() {System.out.println("Generate heat");};

    public abstract void makeNoise();

}
```

This class has an implementation called `generateHeat` and an abstract method called `makeNoise`. Let's also create a class called `Head` that we will use in a composition:

```java
public class Head {

    String size;

    public String getSize() {

        return size;

    }

    public void setSize(String aSize) { size = aSize;};

}
```

Head has two methods: `getSize` and `setSize`.

Now let's create a class called `Dog` that is a subclass of `Mammal`, implements `Nameable`, and has a `Head` object (see Figure 8.5):

```java
public class Dog extends Mammal implements Nameable {

    String name;

    Head head;

    public void makeNoise(){System.out.println("Bark");};

    public void setName (String aName) {name = aName;};
    public String getName () {return (name);};

}
```

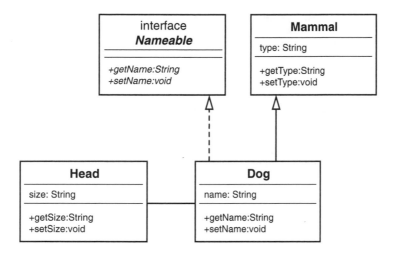

FIGURE 8.5

A UML diagram of the sample code.

In a nutshell Java builds objects in three ways: inheritance, interfaces, and composition. Note the dashed line in Figure 8.5 that represents the interface. This example illustrates when you should use each of these constructs. When do you choose an abstract class? When do you choose an interface? When do you choose composition? Let's explore further.

By now you should be familiar with the following concepts:

- Dog is a Mammal, so the relationship is inheritance.
- Dog implements Nameable, so the relationship is an interface.
- Dog has a Head, so the relationship is composition.

After looking at this UML diagram, you may come up with an obvious question: Even though the dashed line from Dog to Nameable represents an interface, isn't it still inheritance? Good catch! Yes, it is inheritance. So why are there two different ways to model inheritance? This is a good question, and the answers are quite subtle.

First, implementation is not inheritance in the strictest sense (this may get me in trouble in some corners). Although inheritance is a strict is-a relationship, an interface is not.
For example:

- A dog is a mammal.
- A reptile is not a mammal.

Thus, a Reptile class could not inherit from the Mammal class.

8

DESIGNING WITH
INTERFACES AND
ABSTRACT CLASSES

However, an interface transcends the various classes. For example:

- A dog is nameable.
- A lizard is nameable.

You can use the `Nameable` class as an interface for objects that are not at all related. This is the key difference between using an abstract class and using an interface. The abstract class represents some sort of implementation. In fact, we saw that `Mammal` provided a method called `generateHeat`. Even though we do not know what kind of mammal we have, we know that all mammals exhibit some shared behavior, or implementation. However, an interface models only behavior. An interface *never* provides any type of implementation, only behavior. The interface specifies behavior that is the same across classes that conceivably have no connection. Not only is `Dog` nameable, but so are `Car`, `Planet`, and so on.

> **WARNING**
>
> An interface specifies certain behavior, but not the implementation. By implementing the `Nameable` interface, you are saying that you will provide nameable behavior by implementing methods called `getName` and `setName`. How you implement these methods is up to you. All you have to do is provide the methods.

How do we know for sure that interfaces have a true is-a relationship? In the case of Java, we can let the compiler tell us. Consider the following code:

```
Dog D = new Dog();
Head H = D;
```

When this code is run through the compiler, the following error is produced:

```
Test.java:6: Incompatible type for Identifier.
    Can't convert Dog to Head. Head H = D;
```

Obviously, a dog is not a head. However, as expected, the following code works just fine:

```
Dog D = new Dog();
Mammal M = D;
```

This is a true inheritance relationship and it is not surprising that the compiler parses this code cleanly since a dog is a mammal.

Now for the true test of the interface. Is an interface an actual is-a relationship? The compiler thinks so:

```
Dog D = new Dog();
Nameable N = D;
```

This code works fine. So we can safely say that a dog is a nameable entity. This is simple but effective proof that both inheritance and interfaces constitute an is-a relationship.

Making a Contract

Now you should have a good understanding of what abstract classes and interfaces are. The simple rule for defining a contract is to provide an unimplemented method, via either an abstract class or an interface. Thus, when a class is designed with the intent of implementing the contract, it must provide the implementation for the unimplemented methods.

As stated earlier, one of the advantages of a contract is to standardize coding conventions. Let's explore this concept in more detail by providing a good example of what happens when coding standards are not used. In this case there are three classes: `Planet`, `Car`, and `Dog`. Each class implements code to name the entity. However, since they are all implemented separately, each class has different syntax to retrieve the name. Consider the following code for the `Planet` class:

```
public class Planet

    String planetName;

    public void getplanetName() {return planetName;};

}
```

Likewise, the `Car` class may have code like this:

```
public class Car

    String carName;

    public void getCarName() { return carName;};

}
```

And the `Dog` class may have code like this:

```
public class Dog

    String dogName;

    public void getDogName() { return dogName;};

}
```

The obvious problem here is that anyone using these classes would have to look at the documentation (what a horrible thought) to figure out how to retrieve the name in each of these cases. Even though looking at the documentation is not the worst fate in the world, it would be nice if all the classes used in a project (or company) would use the same naming convention—it would make life a bit easier. This is where the Nameable interface comes in.

The idea would be to make a contract for any type of class that needs to use a name. As users of various classes move from one class to the other, they would not have to figure out the current syntax for naming an object. The Planet class, the Car class, and the Dog class would all have the same naming syntax.

To implement this lofty goal, we can create an interface (we can use the Nameable interface that we used previously). The convention is that all classes must implement Nameable. In this way, the users only have to remember a single interface for all classes when it comes to naming conventions:

```
public interface Nameable {

    public String getName();
    public void setName(String aName);

}
```

The new classes, Planet, Car, and Dog, should look like this:

```
public class Planet implements Nameable

    String planetName;

    public String getName() {return planetName;};
    public void setName(String myName) { planetName = myName;};

}

public class Car implements Nameable

    String carName;

    public String getName() {return carName;};
    public void setName(String myName) { carName = myName;};

}

public class Dog implements Nameable
```

```
String dogName;

public String getName() {return dogName;};
public void setName(String myName) { dogName = myName;};

}
```

In this way, we have a standard interface and we have used a contract to ensure that it is the case.

There is one little issue that you may have thought about. The idea of a contract is great as long as everyone plays by the rules, but what if some shady individual does not want to play by the rules? The bottom line is that there is nothing to stop someone from breaking the standard contract; however, in some cases doing so will get them in deep trouble.

On one level, a project manager can insist that everyone use the contract—just like team members must use the same variable naming conventions and configuration management system. If a team member fails to abide by the rules, he or she could be reprimanded or even fired.

Enforcing rules is one way to ensure that contracts are followed, but there are instances in which breaking a contract will result in unusable code. Consider the Java interface `Runnable`. Java applets implement the `Runnable` interface because it requires that any class implementing `Runnable` must implement a `run` method. This is important because the browser in which the applet runs will call the `run` method. If the `run` method does not exist, then things will break.

System Plug-in-Points

Basically, contracts are "plug-in points" into your code. Anyplace where you want to make parts of a system abstract, you can use a contract. Instead of coupling to objects of specific classes, you can connect to any object that implements the contract. You need to be aware of where contracts are useful; however, you can overuse them. You want to identify common features such as the `Nameable` interface, as discussed in this chapter. However, be aware that there is a trade-off when using contracts. They may make code reuse more of a reality, but they make things somewhat more complex.

An E-Business Example

It is sometimes hard to convince a decision maker, who may have no development background, where the monetary savings of code reuse really is. However, when reusing code, it is pretty easy to understand the advantage to the bottom line. In this section we will walk through a simple, but practical example of how to create a workable framework using inheritance, abstract classes, interfaces and composition.

An E-Business Problem

Perhaps the best way to understand the power of reuse is to present an example of how you would reuse code. In this example we'll use inheritance (via interfaces and abstract classes) and composition. Our goal is to create a framework that will make code reuse a reality, reduce coding time, and reduce maintenance—all the typical software development wish list items.

Let's start our own Internet business! It should be easy, if everyone else is doing it. Let's assume that we have a client, a small pizza shop, called Papa's Pizza. Despite the fact that it is a small, family-owned business, Papa realizes that the Web is the wave of the future. Papa wants his customers to access his Web site, find out what Papa's Pizza is all about, and order pizzas right from the comfort of their Java-enabled browsers.

WARNING
While we will state many of the requirements for this example, the code used will only implement a very small subset of the functionality. It is obvious that we cannot implement the entire Web site here. We are only concerned with illustrating how abstract classes and Java interfaces are used to create a framework and take advantage of code reuse.

At the site we develop, customers will be able to bring up the Web site, select the products they want to order, and select a delivery mechanism and time for delivery. They can either eat their food at the restaurant, pick up the order, or have the order delivered. For example, a customer decides at 3:00 that he wants to order a pizza dinner (with salads, breadsticks, and drinks) delivered to his home at 6:00. Let's say the customer is at work (on a break, of course). So he gets on the Web and selects the pizzas, including size, toppings, and crust; the salads, including dressings; breadsticks; and drinks. He chooses the delivery option, and requests that the food be delivered to his home at 6:00. Then he pays for the order by credit card, gets a confirmation number, and exits. Within a few minutes he gets an email confirmation as well. We will set up accounts so that when people bring up the site, they will get a greeting reminding them of who they are, what their favorite pizza is, and what new pizzas have been created this week.

When the system is finally complete, it is deemed a total success. For the next several weeks Papa's customers happily order pizzas and other food and drinks over the Internet. During this rollout period, Papa's brother-in-law, who owns a donut shop called Dad's Donuts, pays Papa a visit. Papa shows Dad the system, and Dad falls in love with it. The next day, Dad calls our company and asks us to develop a Web-based system for his donut shop. This is great, and exactly what we had hoped for. Now how can we leverage the code that we used for the pizza shop in the system for the donut shop?

And how many more small businesses, besides Papa's Pizza and Dad's Donuts, could take advantage of our framework to get on the Web? If we can develop a good, solid framework, then we will be able to efficiently deliver Web-based systems at lower costs than we were able to do before. There will also be an added advantage that the code will have been tested and implemented previously, so debugging and maintenance should be greatly reduced.

The Non-Reuse Approach

There are many reasons the concept of code reuse has not been as successful as some software developers would like. First, many times reuse is not even considered when developing a system. Second, even when reuse is entered into the equation, the issues of schedule constraints, limited resources, and budgetary concerns often short-circuit the best intentions.

In many instances, code ends up highly coupled to the specific application for which it was written. This means that the code within the application is highly dependent on other code within the same application.

A lot of code reuse is the result of simply using cut, copy, and paste operations. While one application is open in a text editor, you would copy code and then paste it into another application. Sometimes certain functions or routines can be used without any change. As is unfortunately many times the case, even though most of the code may remain identical, a small bit of code must change to work in a specific application.

For example, consider two totally separate applications, as represented by the UML diagram in Figure 8.6.

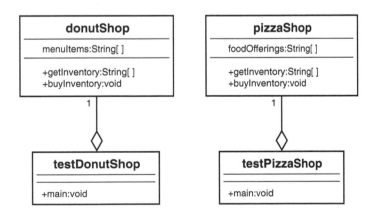

FIGURE 8.6

Applications on Divergent Paths.

8

DESIGNING WITH
INTERFACES AND
ABSTRACT CLASSES

In this example, the applications `testDonutShop` and `testPizzaShop` are totally independent code modules. The code is kept totally separate, and there is no interaction between the modules. However, these applications might use some common code. In fact, some code may have been copied verbatim from one application to another. At some point, someone involved with the project might decide to create a library of these shared pieces of code to use in these and other applications. In many well-run and disciplined projects, this approach works well. Coding standards, configuration management, change management, and so on are all very well run. However, in many instances, this discipline breaks down.

Anyone who is familiar with the software development process knows that when bugs crop up and time is being wasted, there is the temptation to put some fixes or additions into a system that are specific to the application currently in distress. This might fix the problem for the distressed application, but could have unintended, possibly harmful, implications for other applications. Thus, in situations like these, the initially shared code can diverge, and separate code bases must be maintained.

For example, one day Papa's Web site crashes. They call us in a panic, and one of our developers is able to track down the problem. The developer fixes the problem, knowing that the fix works, but is not quite sure why. The developer also does not know what other areas of the system the fix might inadvertently affect. So the developer makes a copy of the code, strictly for use in the Papa's Pizza system. This is affectionately named Version 2.01papa. Since the developer does not yet totally understand the problem, and because Dad's system is working fine, the code is not migrated to the donut shop's system.

TIP

Tracking Down a Bug
The fact that the bug turned up in the pizza system does not mean that it will also turn up in the donut system. Even though the bug caused a crash in the pizza shop, the donut shop may never encounter it. It may be that the fix to the pizza shop's code is more dangerous to the donut shop than the original bug.

The next week Dad calls up in a panic, with a totally unrelated problem. A developer fixes it, again not knowing how the fix will affect the rest of the system, makes a separate copy of the code, and calls it Version 2.03dad. This scenario gets played out for all the sites we now have in operation. So there are a dozen or more copies of the code, with various versions for the various sites. This becomes a mess. We have multiple code paths and have crossed the point of no return. We can never merge them again (well perhaps we could, but from a business perspective, this would be costly).

Our goal is to avoid the mess of the previous example. While many systems must deal with legacy issues, fortunately for us, the pizza and donut applications are brand-new systems. Thus, we can use a bit of foresight and design this system in a reusable manner. In this way we will not run into the maintenance nightmare just described. What we want to do is factor out as much commonality as possible. In our design, we will hone in on all the common business functions that exist in a Web-based application. Instead of having multiple application classes like testPizzaShop and testDonutShop, we can create a design that has a class called Shop that all the applications will use.

Notice that testPizzaShop and testDonutShop have similar interfaces, getInventory and buyInventory. We will factor out this commonality and require that all applications that conform to our Shop framework implement getInventory and buyInventory methods. This requirement to conform to a standard is sometimes called a *contract*. By explicitly setting forth a contract of services, you isolate the code from a single implementation. In Java, you can implement a contract by using an interface or an abstract class. Let's explore how this is accomplished.

An E-Business Solution

Now let's show how to use a contract to factor out some of the commonality of these systems. In this case we will create an abstract class to factor out some of the implementation, and an interface (our familiar Nameable) to factor out some behavior.

Our goal is to provide customized versions of our Web application, with the following features:

- An interface, called Nameable, which is part of the contract.
- An abstract class called Shop, which is also part of the contract.
- A class called CustList, which we use in composition.
- A new implementation of Shop for each customer we service.

The UML Object Model

The newly created Shop class is where the functionality is factored out. Notice in Figure 8.7 that the methods getInventory and buyInventory have been moved up the hierarchy tree from DonutShop and PizzaShop to the abstract class Shop. Now, whenever we want to provide a new, customized version of Shop, we simply plug in a new implementation of Shop (such as a grocery shop). Shop is the contract that the implementations must abide by:

```
public abstract class Shop  {

    CustList customerList;
```

```java
public void CalculateSaleTax() {

    System.out.println("Calculate Sales Tax");

};

public abstract String[] getInventory();

public abstract void buyInventory(String item);

}
```

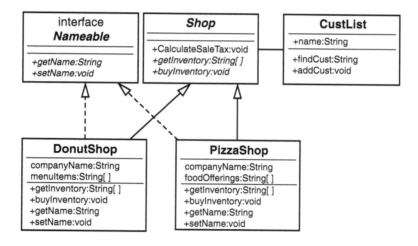

FIGURE 8.7

A UML diagram of the Shop *system.*

To show how composition fits into this picture, the Shop class has a customer list. Thus, the class CustList is contained within Shop:

```java
public class CustList {

    String name;

    public  String findCust() {return name;};
    public  void addCust(String Name){};

}
```

To illustrate the use of an interface in this example, an interface called Nameable is defined:

```
public interface Nameable {

    public abstract String getName();
    public abstract void setName(String name);

}
```

We could potentially have a large number of different implementations, but all the rest of the code (the application) is the same. In this small example, the code savings may not look like a lot. But in a large, real-world application, the code savings is significant. Let's take a look at the donut shop implementation:

```
public class DonutShop extends Shop implements Nameable {

    String companyName;

    String[] menuItems = {
        "Donuts",
        "Muffins",
        "Danish",
        "Coffee",
        "Tea"
};

    public String[] getInventory() {

        return menuItems;

    }

    public void buyInventory(String item) {

        System.out.println("\nYou have just purchased " + item);

    }

    public String getName(){

        return companyName;
    }

    public void setName(String name){

        companyName = name;;
    }
}
```

The pizza shop implementation looks very similar:

```java
public class PizzaShop extends Shop implements Nameable {

    String companyName;


    String[] foodOfferings = {
        "Pizza",
        "Spaghetti",
        "Garden Salad",
        "Anitpasto",
        "Calzone"
    };

    public String[] getInventory() {

        return foodOfferings;

    }

    public void buyInventory(String item) {

        System.out.println("\nYou have just purchased " + item);

    }

    public String getName(){

        return companyName;
    }

    public void setName(String name){

        companyName = name;;
    }

}
```

Unlike the initial case, where there are a large number of customized applications, we now have only a single primary class (`Shop`) and various customized classes (`PizzaShop`, `DonutShop`). There is no coupling between the application and any of the customized classes. The only thing the application is coupled to is the contract (`Shop`). The contract specifies that any implementation of `Shop` must provide an implementation for two methods, `getInventory` and `buyInventory`. It also must provide an implementation for `getName` and `setName` that relates to the interface `Nameable` that is implemented.

Although this solution solves the problem of highly coupled implementations, we still have the problem of deciding which implementation to use. With the current strategy, we would still have to have separate applications. In essence, you have to provide one application for each Shop implementation. Even though we are using the Shop contract, we still have the same situation as before we used the contract:

```
DonutShop myShop= new DonutShop();
```

```
PizzaShop myShop = new PizzaShop ();
```

How do we get around this problem?

We can create objects dynamically. In Java we can use code like this:

```
String className = args[0];
```

```
Shop  myShop;
```

```
myShop = (Shop)Class.forName(className).newInstance();
```

In this case, you set `className` by passing a parameter to the code. (There are other ways to set `className`, such as by using a system property.)

Let's look at Shop using this approach (note that there is no exception handling and nothing else besides object instantiation):

```
class TestShop {

   public static void main (String args[]) {

      Shop shop = null;

      String className = args[0];

      System.out.println("Instantiate the class:" + className + "\n");


      try {

          shop = (Shop)Class.forName(className).newInstance();// new
pizzaShop();

      } catch (Exception e) {

          e.printStackTrace();
      }
```

```
String[] Inventory = shop.getInventory();


// list the inventory

for (int i=0; i<Inventory.length; i++) {
    System.out.println("Argument" + i + " = " + Inventory[i]);
}


// buy an item

shop.buyInventory(Inventory[1]);

    }

}
```

TIP

Compiling This Code

If you who want to compile this Java code, make sure to set `classpath` to the current directory:

```
javac -classpath . Nameable.java
javac -classpath . Shop.java
javac -classpath . CustList.java
javac -classpath . DonutShop.java
javac -classpath . PizzaShop.java
javac -classpath . TestShop.java
```

To run the code to test the pizza shop application, execute the following command:

```
java -classpath . TestShop PizzaShop
```

In this way, we can use the same application code for both PizzaShop and DonutShop. If we add a GroceryShop application, then we only have to provide the implementation and the appropriate string to the main application. No application code needs to change.

Conclusion

When designing classes and object models, it is vitally important to understand how the objects are related to each other. This chapter discusses the primary topics of building object: inheritance, interfaces, and composition. In this chapter you have learned how to build reusable code by designing with contracts.

In Chapter 9, "Building Objects," we complete our O-O journey and explore how objects that may be totally unrelated can interact with each other.

References

Coad, Peter, and Mark Mayfield: *Java Design*. Object International, 1999.

Meyers, Scott: *Effective C++*. Addison-Wesley, 1992.

Building Objects

IN THIS CHAPTER

- Learn how to build objects using other objects
- Delve deeper into the tradeoffs between functionality versus complexity
- Understand how objects relate to each other
- Learn how to determine cardinality

The previous two chapters cover the topics of inheritance and composition. In Chapter 7, "Mastering Inheritance and Composition" we learned that inheritance and composition represent the primary ways to build objects. In Chapter 8, "Frameworks and Reuse: Designing with Interfaces and Abstract Classes," we learned that there are varying degrees of inheritance and how inheritance, interfaces, abstract classes, and composition all fit together.

This chapter covers the issue of how objects are related to each other. Now, you may say that this topic was already introduced, and you would be correct. Both inheritance and composition represent ways that objects interact. In fact, the pure nature of inheritance means that one class inherits from another class, thus there must be some level of interaction.

Well, yes and no. Although it is true that inheritance is a relationship between two classes, what is really happening is that a wholly new class is created. Let's revisit the example of the Person and Employee classes (see Figure 9.1).

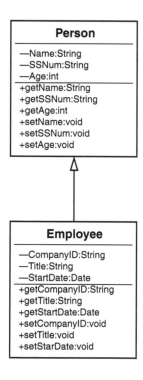

FIGURE 9.1

An inheritance relationship.

Although there are indeed two classes here, the relationship is not interaction—it is inheritance. Basically, an employee is a person. An `Employee` object does not send a message to a `Person` object. An `Employee` object does need the services of a `Person` object. This is because an `Employee` object is a `Person` object.

However, composition is a different situation. Composition represents an interaction between various objects. So whereas Chapter 8 covers the different flavors of inheritance, this chapter delves into the various flavors of composition and how objects interact with each other.

Composition Relationships

We have already seen that composition represents a part of a whole. Whereas the inheritance relationship is stated in terms of is-a, composition is stated in terms of has-a. We know intuitively that a car *has an* engine (see Figure 9.2).

WARNING

Please forgive my grammar. For consistency, I will stick with *has a* engine even though *has an* engine may be better grammar.

A Car has a Steering Wheel

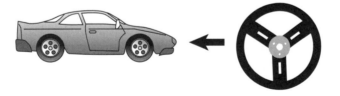

FIGURE 9.2

A composition relationship.

The reason for using composition is that it combines systems into less complex parts. This is a common way for people to approach problems. Studies show that even the best of us can keep, at most, seven *chunks* of data in our short-term memory at one time. Thus we like to use abstract concepts. Instead of saying that we have a large unit with a steering wheel, four tires, an engine, and so on, we say that we have a car. This makes it easier for us to communicate and keep things clear in our heads.

Composition also helps in other ways, such as making parts interchangeable. If all steering wheels are the same, it does not matter which steering wheel goes with which car. In software development, interchangeable parts mean reuse. In chapters 7 and 8 of their book *Object-Oriented Design in Java,* Stephen Gilbert and Bill McCarty present many examples of associations and composition in much more detail. I highly recommend referencing this material for a more in depth look into these subjects. Here we address some of the more fundamental points of these concepts and explore some variations of their examples.

Building in Phases

Another major advantage in using composition is that systems and subsystems can be built independently and perhaps more importantly, tested independently.

There is no question that today's software systems are quite complex. To build quality software, you must follow one overriding rule to be successful: Keep things as simple as possible. For large software systems to work properly and be easily maintained, they must be broken up into smaller, more manageable parts. How do you accomplish this? On page 254 of their book, Stephen Gilbert and Bill McCarty reference an article published in 1962 titled "The Architecture of Complexity" by Nobel prize winner Herbert Simon. Dr. Simon included the following thoughts regarding stable systems:

- Stable complex systems usually take the form of a hierarchy, where each system is built from simpler subsystems, and each subsystem is built from simpler subsystems still. You may already be familiar with this principle because it forms the basis for functional decomposition, the method behind procedural software development. In object-oriented design, you apply the same principles to composition—building complex objects from simpler pieces.

- Stable, complex systems are *nearly decomposable*. This means that you can identify the parts that make up the system and can tell the difference between interactions between the parts and inside the parts. Stable systems have fewer links between their parts than they do inside their parts. Thus, a modular stereo system, with simple links between the speakers, turntable, and amplifier, is inherently more stable than an integrated system, which isn't easily decomposable.

- Stable complex systems are almost always composed of only a few different kinds of subsystems, arranged in different combinations. Those subsystems, in turn, are generally composed of only a few different kinds of parts.

- Stable systems that work have almost always evolved from simple systems that worked. Rather than build a new system from scratch—reinventing the wheel—the new system builds on the proven designs that went before it.

In our stereo example (see Figure 9.3), suppose that the stereo system was totally integrated and was not built from components (that is, that the stereo system was one, big black box system). In this case, what would happen if the CD player broke and became unusable? You would have to take in the entire system for repair. Not only would this be more complicated and expensive, but you would not have the use of any of the other components.

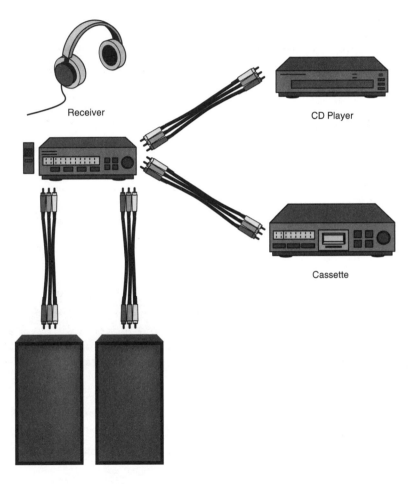

FIGURE 9.3
Building, testing, and verifying a complete system one step at a time.

If the system were components rather than a single unit, if the CD player broke, you could disconnect the CD player and simply take it for repair (note that all the components are connected by patch cords). This would obviously be less complicated and less expensive, and it would take less time than having to deal with a single unit. As an added benefit, you could still use the rest of the system. You could even buy another CD player since it is a component. The repair person could then plug your broken CD player into his repair systems to test and fix it. All in all, the component approach works quite well. Composition is one of the primary weapons that you, as a software designer, have in your arsenal to fight software complexity.

One major advantage of using components is that you can use components that were built by other developers or even third party vendors. However, using a software component from another source requires a certain amount of trust. Third-party components must come from a reliable source and you must feel comfortable that the software is properly tested and will perform the advertised functions properly. There are still many who would rather build their own than trust components built by others.

Types of Composition

Generally, there are two types of composition: association and aggregation. In both cases these relationships represent collaborations between the objects. The stereo example we just used to explain one of the primary advantages of composition actually represents an association.

TIP

Is Composition a Form of Association?

Composition is another area in O-O technologies where there is a question of what came first, the chicken or the egg. Some texts say that composition is a form of association, and some say that an association is a form of composition. In any event, in this book, we consider inheritance and composition the two primary ways of building classes. Thus, in this book, an association is a form of composition.

All forms of composition include a has-a relationship. However, there are differences between associations and aggregations based on how you visualize the parts of the whole. In an aggregation you normally see only the whole, and in associations you normally see the parts that make up the whole.

Aggregations

Perhaps that most intuitive form of composition is aggregation. *Aggregation* means that a complex object is composed of other objects. A TV set is a clean, neat package that you use for entertainment. When you look at your TV you see a single TV. Most of the time, you do not stop and think about the fact that the TV contains some transistors, a picture tube, a tuner, and so on. Sure, you do see a switch to turn the set on and off, and you certainly see the picture tube. However, this is not the way people normally think of TVs. When you go into an appliance store, the salesperson does not say, "Let me show you this aggregation of transistors, a picture tube, a tuner, and so on." He says, "Let me show you this TV."

Similarly, when you go to buy a car, you do not pick and choose all the individual components of the car. You do not decide what sparkplugs to buy or what door handles to buy. You go to buy a car. Of course, you do choose some options, but for the most part, you choose the car as a whole, a complex object made up of many other complex and simple objects (see Figure 9.4).

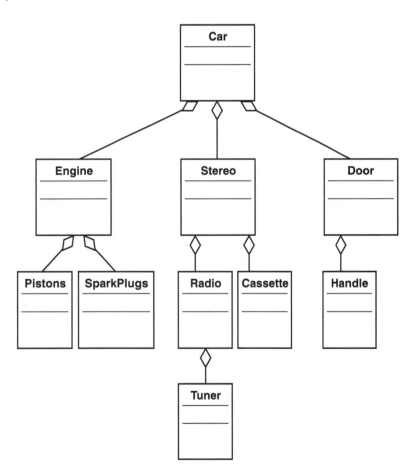

FIGURE 9.4

An aggregation hierarchy for a car.

Associations

Whereas aggregations represent relationships where you normally only see the whole, *associations* present both the whole and the parts. As stated in the stereo example, the various components are presented separately and connect to the whole by use of *patch cords (the cords that connect the various components)*. Each one of the stereo components has its own user interface and is manipulated separately. We can look back at the example in Chapter 2, "How to Think in Terms of Objects," at the example of designing for minimal interfaces.

In this example (see Figure 9.5), the whole is the computer system. The components are the monitor, keyboard, mouse, and main box. Each is a separate object, but together they represent the whole of the computer system. The main computer is using the keyboard, the mouse, and the monitor to delegate some of the work. In other words, the computer box needs the service of a mouse, but does not have the capability to provide this service by itself. Thus, the computer box requests the service from a separate mouse via the specific port and cable connecting the mouse to the box.

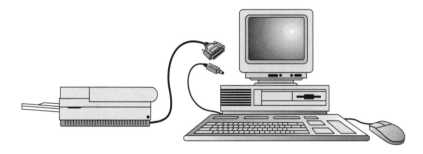

FIGURE 9.5
Associations.

TIP

Aggregation Versus Association

An aggregation is a complex object composed of other objects. An association is used when one object wants another object to perform a service for it.

Using Associations and Aggregations Together

One thing that you might have noticed in all the examples is that the dividing lines between what is an association and what is an aggregation are blurred. Suffice it to say that many of your most interesting design decision will come down to whether to use associations or aggregations.

For example, the computer system example used to describe association also contains some aggregation. While the interaction between the computer box, the monitor, the keyboard, and the mouse is association, the computer box itself represents aggregation. You see only the computer box, but it is actually a complex system made up of other objects, including chips, motherboards, video cards, and so on.

Similarly, in the stereo example, the relationship between the receiver, the speakers, and the CD player is association; however, each of these components are complex objects that are made up of other objects.

In the car example, while the engine, sparkplugs, and doors represent composition, the stereo also represents an association relationship.

> **TIP**
>
> ### No One Right Answer
> As usual, there is not one absolutely correct answer when it comes to making a design decision. Design is not an exact science. Although we can make general rules to live by, these rules are not hard and fast.

9

Avoiding Dependencies

When using composition, it is desirable to avoid making objects highly dependent on one another. One way to make objects very dependent on each other is to mix domains. In the best of all worlds, an object in one domain should not be mixed with an object in another domain. We can return again to the stereo example to explain this concept.

By keeping the receiver and the CD player in separate domains, the stereo system is easier to use. For example, if the CD component breaks, you can send the CD player off to be repaired individually. In this case the CD player and the cassette player have separate domains. This provides flexibility such as buying the CD player and the cassette player from separate manufacturers. So if you decide that you want to swap out the CD player with a brand from another manufacturer, you can.

Sometimes there is a certain convenience in mixing domains. A good example of this pertains to the existence of TV/VCR combinations. Granted, it is convenient to have both in the same module. However, if the TV breaks, the VCR is unusable—at least as part of the unit it was purchased in.

In fact, anyone who has kids and has discovered the wonder of the TV/VCR combination can attest to this dilemma. On long trips, we can take the unit into the car and let the kids watch their favorite videos, thus keeping the incessant chanting of "are we there yet" to a minimum. When we are not travelling, which is most of the time, the TV part of the unit is used in the exercise room to pass the time while doing our daily workouts. Unfortunately, on at least two occasions over the years, the VCR part of the unit has broken. This has forced us to take the entire unit to the repair shop. Since the TV is integrated with the VCR, the TV part is obviously unavailable for use while the unit is out for repair. Thus, our exercise time does not pass as quickly. If the TV and VCR were separate components, then we could at least use the TV while the VCR is out for repair.

You need to determine whether you want convenience or stability. There is no right answer. It all depends on the application and the environment. In the case of the TV/VCR combination, we decided that the convenience of the integrated unit (for use in travel) far outweighed the risk of lower unit stability (see Figure 9.6).

More Convenient/Less Stable

TV part

FIGURE 9.6
Convenience versus stability.

TIP

Mixing Domains

Again, the convenience of mixing domains is a design decision. If the power of having a TV/VCR combination outweighs the risk and potential downtime of the individual components, then mixing of domains may well be the preferred design choice.

Cardinality

Stephen Gilbert and Bill McCarty describe Cardinality as the number of objects that participate in an association and whether the participation is optional or mandatory. To determine Cardinality ask the following questions:

- Which objects collaborate with which other objects?
- How many objects participate in each collaboration?
- Is the collaboration optional or mandatory?

For example, let's consider the following example. We are creating an `Employee` class that inherits from `Person` and has relationships with the following classes:

- `Division`
- `JobDescription`
- `Spouse`
- `Child`

What do these classes do? Are they optional? How many does an `Employee` need?

- `Division`
    - This object contains the information relating to the division that the employee works for.
    - Each employee must work for a division, so the relationship is mandatory.
    - The employee works for one, and only one, division.
- `JobDescription`
    - This object contains a job description most likely containing information such as salary grade and salary range.
    - Each employee must have a job description, so the relationship is mandatory.

- The employee can hold various jobs during the tenure at a company. Thus, an employee can have many job descriptions. These descriptions can be kept as a history if an employee changes jobs, or it is possible that an employee may hold two different jobs at one time. For example, a supervisor may take on an employee's responsibilities if the employee quits and a replacement has not yet been hired.

- Spouse

  - In this simplistic example the Spouse class contains only the anniversary date.

  - An employee can be married or not married. Thus, a spouse is optional.

  - An employee can have only one spouse.

- Child

  - In this simple example the Child class contains only the string FavoriteToy.

  - An employee can have children or not have children.

  - An employee can have no children or an infinite number of children (wow!). You could make a design decision as to the upper limit of the number of children that the system can handle.

To sum up, the following represents the Cardinality of the associations of the classes we just considered:

Association	Cardinality	Optional/ Mandatory
Employee/Division	1	Mandatory
Employee/JobDescription	1..n	Mandatory
Employee/Spouse	0..1	Optional
Employee/Child	0..n	Optional

TIP

Cardinality Notation

The notation of 0..1 means that an employee can have either zero or one spouse. The notation of 0..n means that an employee can have any number of children from zero to an unlimited number. The n basically represents infinity.

Figure 9.7 shows the class diagram for this system. Note that in this class diagram the Cardinality is indicated along the association lines. Refer to the table above to see whether the association is mandatory or not.

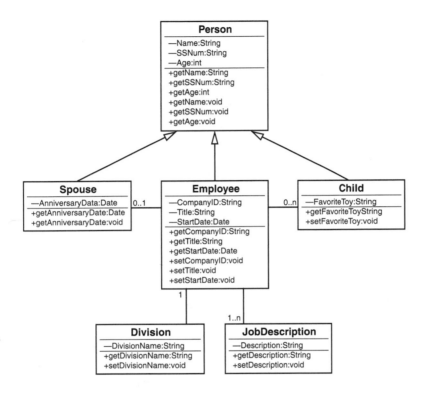

FIGURE 9.7

Cardinality in a UML diagram.

How do we represent an association that may contain multiple objects (like 0 to many children) in code?

Here is the code for the Employee class:

```
import java.util.Date;

public class Employee extends Person{

        private String CompanyID;
        private String Title;
        private Date StartDate;
```

```
        private Spouse spouse;
        private Child[] child;
        private Division division;
        private JobDescription[] jobDescriptions;

        public String getCompanyID() {return CompanyID;};
        public String getTitle() {return Title;};
        public Date getStartDate() {return StartDate;};

        public void setCompanyID(String CompanyID) {};
        public void setTitle(String Title) {};
        public void setStartDate(int StartDate) {};

}
```

Note that the classes that have a one-to-many relationship are represented by arrays in the code:

```
private Child[] child;
private JobDescription[] jobDescriptions;
```

Optional Associations

One of the most important issues when dealing with associations is to make sure that your application is designed to check for optional associations. This means that your code must check to see if the association is null.

Suppose that in the previous example, your code assumes that every employee has a spouse. However, if one employee is not married, then the code will have a problem (see Figure 9.8). If your code does indeed expect a spouse to exist, then it may well fail and leave the system in an unstable state. The bottom line is that the code must check for a null condition, and must handle this as a valid condition.

Tying It All Together: An Example

Let's work on a simple example that will tie the concepts of inheritance, interfaces, composition, associations, and aggregations together into a single, short system diagram.

Consider the example used in Chapter 8, with one addition: We will add an Owner class that will take the dog out for walks.

Recall that the Dog class inherits directly from the Mammal class. This is represented by the solid arrow from the Dog class to the Mammal class. The Nameable class is an interface that Dog implements, which is represented by the dashed arrow from the Dog class to the Nameable interface.

Object Mary

FIGURE 9.8

Checking all optional associations.

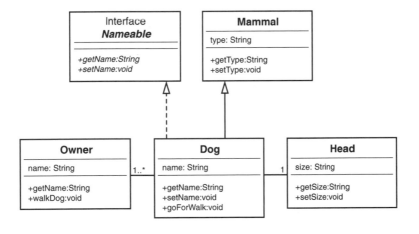

FIGURE 9.9

A UML diagram for the Dog *example.*

In this chapter we are mostly concerned with associations and aggregations. The relationship between the Dog class and the Head class is considered aggregation because the head is actually part of the dog. The Cardinality on the line connecting the two class diagrams specifies that a dog can have only a single head.

The relationship between the Dog class and the Owner class is association. The owner is clearly not part of the dog, or vice versa, so we can safely eliminate aggregation. However, the dog does require a service from the owner—the act of taking him on a walk. The cardinality on the line connecting the Dog and Owner classes specifies that a dog can have one or more owners (for example, a wife and husband can both be considered owners, with shared responsibility for walking the dog).

These relationships—inheritance, interfaces, composition, associations, and aggregations—represent the bulk of the design work that you will encounter when designing O-O systems.

Conclusion

In this chapter we have explored some of the finer points of composition and its two primary types: aggregation and association. Whereas inheritance represents a new kind of an already existing object, composition represents the interactions between various objects.

The last three chapters have covered the basics of inheritance and composition. Using these concepts and your skills in the software development process, you are on your way to designing solid classes and object models.

This book has covered a lot of material. The intent is to provide a high-level overview to the concepts involved in the O-O thought process. Hopefully this book has whetted your appetite for this subject and you will seek out other books that go into far more detail. Many of the individual topics covered in this book—such as UML and use cases—have complete books devoted to them. Good hunting!

References

Gilbert, Stephen, and Bill McCarty: *Object-Oriented Design in Java*. The Waite Group, 1998.

Coad, Peter, and Mark Mayfield: *Java Design*. Object International, 1999.

Meyers, Scott: *Effective C++*. Addison-Wesley, 1992.

An Overview of UML Used in This Book

This appendix is a brief overview of the UML notation used in this book. It is not a comprehensive tutorial on UML because that would require an entire book unto itself (and there are many such books). Because this book is a fundamentals book, the UML that is used only scratches the surface of what UML actually offers.

In this book, the UML notation that we are concerned with includes class diagrams and Class-Responsibility-Collaboration (CRC) modeling. Many of the more advanced components of UML are not used in this book. Each of those components could warrant a complete chapter or more. Again, the purpose of this appendix is to provide a quick overview of class diagrams so that if you are unfamiliar with class diagrams, you can pick up the basics quickly and so the examples in the book are more meaningful.

What Is UML?

UML, as its name implies, is a modeling language. The *UML User Guide* defines UML as "a graphical language for visualizing, specifying, constructing and documenting the artifacts of a software-intensive system." The UML gives you a standard way to write the system's blueprints. In a nutshell, UML offers a way to graphically represent and manipulate an object-oriented (O-O) software system. It is not only the representation of the design of a system, but a tool to assist in this design.

However, it is important not to link UML and O-O development too closely. In his article "What the UML Is—and Isn't", Craig Larman states, "Yet unfortunately, in the context of software engineering and the UML diagramming language, acquiring the skills to read and write UML notation seems to sometimes be equated with skill in object-oriented analysis and design. Of course, this is not so, and the latter is much more important than the former. Therefore, I recommend seeking education and educational materials in which intellectual skill in object-oriented analysis and design is paramount rather than UML notation or the use of a case tool" (p. 20).

Although UML is very important, it is much more important to learn the O-O skills first. Learning UML before learning O-O concepts is similar to learning how to read an electrical diagram without first knowing anything about electricity.

The Structure of a Class Diagram

A class diagram is constructed of three different parts: the class name, the attributes, and the methods (constructors are considered methods). The class diagram is essentially a rectangle that separates these three parts with horizontal lines. The book often uses a cabbie metaphor as an illustration. Figure A.1 shows the UML class diagram representing this class.

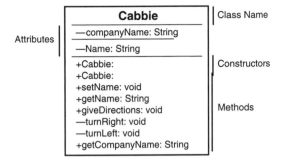

FIGURE A.1

A UML Diagram of the Cabbie *class.*

This UML diagram corresponds exactly to the following Java code:

```
/*

    This class defines a cabbie and assigns a cab

*/
public class Cabbie {

    // Place the name of the company here
    private static String companyName = "Blue Cab Company";

    // Name of the cabbie
    private String Name;

    // Car assigned to cabbie

    // Default constructor for the cabbie
    public Cabbie() {

        Name = null;
        myCab = null;

    }

    // Name initializing the constructor for the cabbie
    public Cabbie(String iName, String serialNumber) {

        Name = iName;
        myCab = new Cab(serialNumber);

    }
```

```
    // Set the name of the cabbie
    public void setName(String iName) {
        Name = iName;
    }

    // Get the name of the cabbie
    public String getName() {
        return Name;
    }

    // Give the cabbie directions
    public void giveDirections(){
    }

    // Cabbie turns right
    private void turnRight(){
    }

    // Cabbie turns left
    private void turnLeft() {
    }

    // Get the name of the company
    public static String getCompanyName() {
        return companyName;
    }

}
// Get the name of the cabbie
```

Take a moment to look at the code and compare it to the UML class diagram. Notice how the class name, attributes, and methods in the code relate to the designation in the class diagram. Really, that is all there is to the class diagram as far as the structure goes. However, there is a lot more information to be gleaned from the diagram. This information is discussed in the following sections.

Attributes and Methods

Besides presenting the structure of the class, the class diagram also presents information about the attributes and methods.

Attributes

Normally, attributes are not thought of as having signatures; methods get all the credit. However, an attribute has a type, and this type is represented in the class diagram. Consider the two attributes that are in the Cabbie example:

```
-companyName:String
-Name:String
```

Both of these attributes are defined as strings. This is represented by the name of the attribute followed by the type (in these cases String). There could have been attributes that were defined as int and float as well, as in this example:

```
-companyNumber:float
-companyAge:int
```

By looking at the class diagram, you can tell the type of the parameter.

Methods

The same logic used with attributes works for methods. Rather than express the type, the diagram shows the return type of the method.

If you look at the following snippet from the Cabbie example, you can see that the name of the method is presented, along with the return type and the access modifier (for example, public, private):

```
+Cabbie:
+giveDirections:void
+getCompanyName:String
```

As you can see here, in all three cases the access modifier is public (designated by the plus sign). If a method were private, there would be a minus sign. Each method name is followed by a colon that separates the method name from the return type.

It is possible to include a parameter list, in the following manner:

```
+getCompanyName(parameter-list):String
```

The parameters in the parameter list are separated by commas.

```
+getCompanyName(parameter1, parameter2, parameter3):String
```

Access Designations

As mentioned previously, the plus signs (+) and minus signs (-) to the left of the attributes and methods signify whether the attributes and methods are public or private. The attribute or method is considered private if there is a minus sign. This means that no other class can access the attribute or method; only methods in the class can inspect or change it.

If the attribute or method has a plus sign to the left, the attribute or method is public, and any class can inspect or modify it. For example, consider the following:

```
-companyNumber:float
+companyAge:int
```

In this example, `companyNumber` is private, and only methods of its class can do anything with it. However, `companyAge` is public and thus it is fair game for any class to access and modify it.

If no access designation is present in the code, the system considers the access to be the default, and no plus or minus is used:

```
companyNumber:float
companyAge:int
```

Protected Access

In Java the default type of access is protected. Protected access means that only classes in the package can access the attribute or method. A Java package is a collection of related classes that are intentionally grouped together by the developer.

Inheritance

To understand how inheritance is represented, consider the `Dog` example presented in Chapter 7, "Mastering Inheritance and Composition." In this example the class `GoldenRetriever` inherits from the class `Dog`. This relationship is represented in UML by a line with an arrowhead pointing in the direction of the parent or superclass.

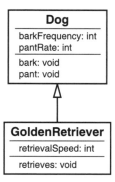

FIGURE A.2
UML diagram of the Dog Hierarchy.

The notation is straightforward, and when the line with the arrowhead is encountered, an inheritance relationship is indicated.

Indicating Interface Inheritance

A dashed line with an arrowhead indicates an interface, which is discussed in the next section.

Because Java is used for the examples in this book, we do not have to worry about multiple inheritance. However, several subclasses can inherit from the same superclass. Again, we can use the Dog example from Chapter 7 (see Figure A.3).

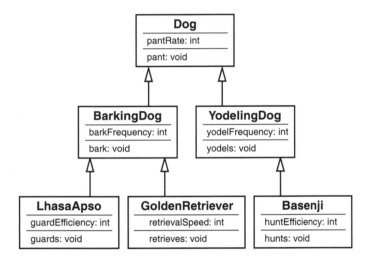

FIGURE A.3

UML diagram of the Expanded Dog Hierarchy.

This example illustrates two concepts when modeling an inheritance tree. First, a superclass can have more than one subclass. Second, the inheritance tree can extend for more than one level. The example in Figure A.3 shows three levels. We could add further levels by adding specific types of retrievers or even adding higher level by creating a Canine class (see Figure A.4).

Interfaces

Because interfaces are a special type of inheritance, the notations are similar and can cause some confusion. Earlier we said that inheritance is represented by a line with an arrowhead. An interface is also represented by a line with an arrowhead—but the arrowhead is connected

to a dashed line. This notation indicates the relationship between inheritance and interfaces, but also differentiates them. Take a look at Figure A.5, which is an abbreviated version of an example in Chapter 8, "Frameworks and Reuse: Designing with Interfaces and Abstract Classes." The Dog class inherits from the class Mammal and implements the interface Nameable.

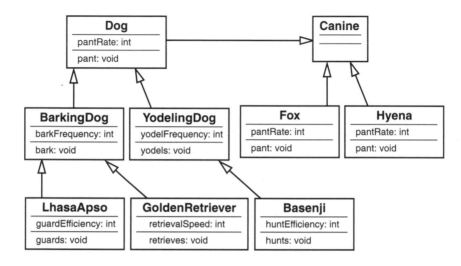

FIGURE A.4
UML diagram of the Canine Hierarchy.

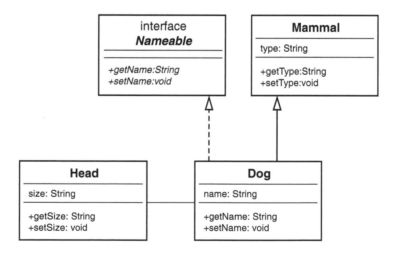

FIGURE A.5
UML Diagram Showing an Interface Relationship.

Composition

Composition indicates that a has-a relationship is being used. When inheritance is not the proper design choice (because the is-a relationship is not appropriate), composition is normally used.

Chapter 9, "Building Objects," talks about two different types of composition: aggregations and associations. Composition is used when classes are built with other classes. This can happen with aggregation, when a class is actually a component of another class (as a tire is to a car). Or it can happen with association, when a class needs the services of another class (for example, when a client needs the services of a server).

Aggregations

An aggregation is represented by a line with a diamond at the head. In the car example of chapter 9, to represent that a steering wheel is part of a car, you use the notation shown in Figure A.6.

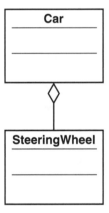

FIGURE A.6

UML Diagram Representing Composition.

As with the inheritance tree, there is no limit (theoretically) to the number of levels of aggregation you can represent. In the Figure A.7 example, there are four levels. Notice that the various levels can represent various aggregations. For example, while a stereo is part of the car, the radio is part of the stereo and the tuner is part of the radio.

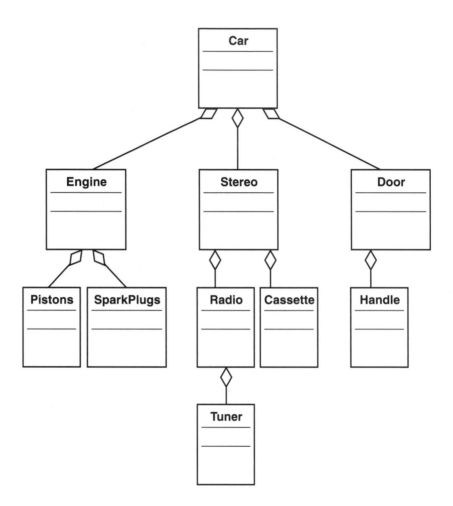

FIGURE A.7
An Expanded Composition UML Diagram.

Associations

While aggregations represent parts of a whole, meaning that one class is logically built with parts of another, associations are simply services provided between classes.

As mentioned earlier, a client/server relationship fits this model. Although it is obvious that a client is not part of a server, and likewise a server is not part of a client, they both depend on each other. In most cases you can say that a server provides the client a service. In UML notation, this service is represented by a plain line, with no shape on either end (see Figure A.8).

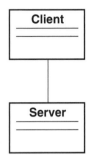

FIGURE A.8

UML Diagram Representing an Association.

Note that because there is no shape on either end of the line, there is no indication about which way the service flows. The figure shows only that there is an association between the two classes.

To illustrate, consider the example of the computer system from Chapter 9, "Building Objects." In this case, there are multiple components, such as a computer, monitor, scanner, keyboard, and mouse. Each of these are totally separate components that interact, to some degree, with the computer itself (see Figure A.9).

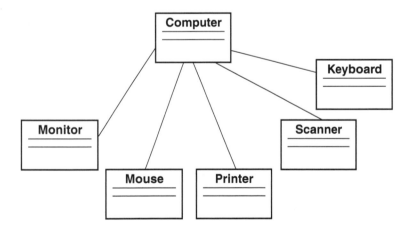

FIGURE A.9

An Expanded UML Diagram Representing Association.

The important thing to note here is that the monitor is technically part of the computer. If you were to create a class for a computer system, you could model it by using aggregation. However, the computer represents some form of aggregation as it is made up of a mother-board, RAM, and so on (see Figure A.10).

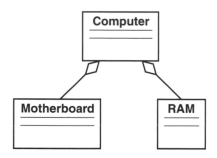

FIGURE A.10
UML Representation of Aggregation.

Cardinality

The last issue to visit in this appendix is cardinality. Basically, *cardinality* pertains to the range of objects that correspond to the class. Using the earlier computer example, we can say that a computer is made up of one, and only one, motherboard. This cardinality is represented as 1. There is no way that a computer can be without a motherboard and, in PCs today, no computer has more than one. On the other hand, a computer must have at least 1 RAM chip, but it may have as many chips as the machine can hold. Thus, we can represent the cardinality as $1..n$, where n represents an unlimited value.

> ## Limited Cardinality Values
> If we know that there are slots for six RAM chips, the upper limit number is not unlimited. Thus, the n would be replaced by a 6, and the cardinality would be 1..6.

Consider the example shown in Figure A.11, from Chapter 9.

In this example, we have several different representations of cardinality. First, the `Employee` class has an association with the `Spouse` class. Based on conventional rules, an employee can have either no spouses or one spouse (at least in our culture, an employee cannot have more than one spouse). Thus, the cardinality of this association is represented as 0..1.

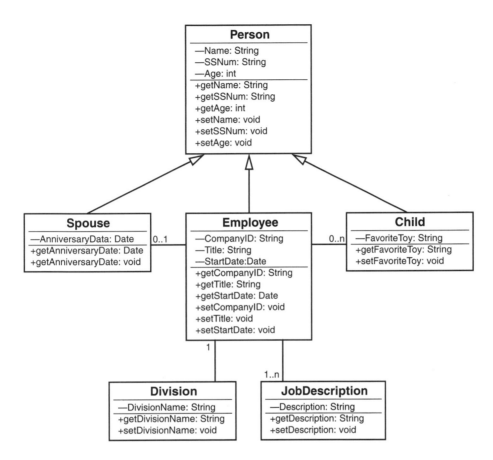

FIGURE A.11

UML Diagram Showing Cardinality.

Making Design Decisions

When designing software, it is important to be sensitive to the fact that there are many different cultures in the world. Thus, making an assumption such as our assumption that an employee can have only one spouse may not be a good thing. If you intend your system to be used internationally, or even nationally within subcultures, you need to think about the design from many angles.

The association between the Employee class and the Child class is somewhat different in that an employee has no theoretical limits to the number of children that the employee can have. Although it is true that an employee may have no children, if the employee does have children, there are no limits to the number of children that the employee may have. Thus, the cardinality of this association is represented as 0..*n*, and again, *n* means that there is no upper limit to the number of children that the system can handle.

As for the relationship between the Employee class and the Division class, this relationship states that each employee can be associated with one, and only one, division. This association is represented by a simple 1.

More Design Issues

In certain situations, it is possible for an employee to be associated with more than one division. For example, a college may allow an individual to hold positions is the mathematics department and the computer science department concurrently. This is another design issue you must consider.

The last cardinality association we will discuss is the association between the Employee class and the JobDescription class. In this system it is possible for an employee to have an unlimited number of job descriptions. However, unlike the Child class, where there can be zero children, in this system there must be at least one job description per employee. Thus, the cardinality of this association is represented as 1..*n*. The association involves is at least one job description per employee, but possibly more (in this case, an unlimited number).

Keeping History

You must also consider that an employee can have job descriptions for past jobs as well as for current jobs. In this case there needs to be a way to differentiate current job descriptions from past ones.

Conclusion

This appendix gives a very brief overview of the UML notation used in this book. As stated in the introduction, UML is a very complex and important topic, and the complete coverage of UML requires a book (or several) unto itself.

UML is used to illustrate O-O examples throughout this book. You do not need UML to design O-O systems, but UML is a tool that can be used to assist in the development of O-O systems.

Learning UML in detail is one of the steps that you should take *after* you are comfortable with the underlying O-O concepts. However, as happens so many times, the chicken and the egg conundrum presents itself. In an effort to illustrate some of the examples in the book, it is very useful to use UML.

It is good to introduce a little of a modeling language (such as UML) and a little of a programming language (such as Java) while explaining O-O concepts. We could, of course, have used C++ instead of Java, and another modeling system rather than UML. It is important to keep in mind that whatever examples you use, you should stay focused on the O-O concepts themselves.

References

Flower, Martin: *UML Distilled*. Addison Wesley Longman, 1997.

Larman, Craig: "What the UML Is—and Isn't," *Java Report*, 4(5):20–24, May 1999.

Booch, G., I. Jacobson, and J. Rumbaugh: *The UML Users Guide*. Addison-Wesley, 1998.

The Evolution of Object-Oriented Languages

This appendix briefly describes the evolution of object-oriented (O-O) programming languages. Surprisingly, although many people believe that O-O technologies are fairly new, O-O languages have their origins in the early 1960s. In fact, much of the history of structured and O-O programming overlaps to some degree.

O-O Languages

What really makes a programming language an O-O language? And when did the O-O movement really start? Many people point to the early 1960s as the time whenSimula-67 introduced the concept of an object.

As the name implies, Simula was created to aid in simulations. It is not a coincidence that simulations typically model real-world systems. Many of these real-world systems contained hundreds, or thousands, of interacting parts. We will follow O-O language evolution through the discussion of several O-O languages. Many point to Smalltalk as the first pure O-O language. Interestingly enough, C++, perhaps the first major commercial O-O success, is not truly O-O. And finally, we will talk about why Java was released with such fanfare and what makes its proponents consider it a complete programming language package.

Simula

By the 1960s programmers realized that programming systems needed to be broken up into small, manageable pieces. The introduction of Simula-67 brought with it the first true programming object, classes and a form of inheritance; therefore, Simula is an important milestone in any discussion on O-O programming languages. The language was designed by Dahl, Myhrhaug and Nygaard at the Norwegian Computing Center at Oslo, Norway. The initial version of the language, Simula-1, was introduced in 1966. The programming modules defined by Simula were based not on procedures, but on actual physical objects. Simula had a novel way of presenting the object, so that each object has its own behavior and data.

Smalltalk

Many consider that the first truly O-O language was Smalltalk, developed at the Learning Research Group at Xerox's Palo Alto Research Center in the early 1970s. In Smalltalk, everything is really an object that enforces the O-O paradigm. It is literally impossible to write a program in Smalltalk that is not O-O. This is not the case for other languages that support objects, such as C++ and Visual Basic (and Java for that matter).

> ### C++ and Java Are Not Purely O-O
> C++ has O-O features, but you can use non-objects in C++. Java is mostly O-O, but the primitive data types, like integers and floats, are not implemented objects.

Smalltalk is actually much more than a programming language: It is a programming environment. In fact, Smalltalk is an interactive environment that interprets code on-the-fly. You can actually change the parameters—and code—of a program while the program is running.

Smalltalk first introduced many other concepts that would later appear revolutionary when implemented in other applications, such as browsers, windows, and pop-up menus. From the O-O perspective, Smalltalk supported inheritance and the concept of sending messages between objects. Smalltalk gained a loyal and vocal following, but initially did not make major gains in the programming market.

C++

Although Smalltalk gave O-O development a certain amount of legitimacy in the marketplace, it took C++ to bring O-O development what it really needed: widespread acceptance in the marketplace. For this reason, C++ may well be the most important O-O language. Not until C++ was released and the industry started supported it with a vengeance did O-O development become mainstream.

C++ has its roots in a project to simulate software running on a distributed system. This simulator, actually written in Simula, is where Bjarne Stroustrup conceived of the idea of combining some of the features of Simula with the syntax of C.

While working at Bell, Stroustrup made personal contacts with the people such as Brian Kernighan and Dennis Ritchie, who wrote the definitive book on C. When the initial simulator written in Simula failed, Stroustrup decided to rewrite it in a C predecessor called BCPL.

C++ was originally implemented in 1982 under the name C with Classes. As the name suggests, the most important concept of C with Classes was the addition of the class. The class concept provided the encapsulation now requisite with O-O languages.

The reasons C++'s O-O roots are in Simula are obvious. However, why did Stroustrup decide to use C? Because, he said, C is flexible, efficient, available, and portable. Some of these points can be debated today, but at the time, these reasons were valid. Perhaps the most important reason he used C was because he was at Bell Labs and C had gained a large following and was widely accepted in the marketplace.

Commercial C++ compilers began to appear in 1988. In June 1989, C++ Release 2.0 legitimately moved C++ into the mainstream of software development; in late 1989 the ANSI C++ committee formed.

While C provided a solid foundation for C++, it also was a bit of a boat anchor. Using C syntax provided a clear transition path from C to C++; however, making C++ backward compatible with C has a serious drawback. C++ did provide O-O constructs; however, it was possible to program in C++ and not even use O-O concepts. Thus, C++ is not considered a true O-O language, but a hybrid language. In short, you can use a C++ compiler and not conform to accepted O-O programming rules.

Java

Java's origins are in consumer electronics. In 1991 Sun Microsystems began to investigate how it might exploit this growing market. Some time later, James Gosling was investigating the possibility of creating a hardware-independent software platform for just this purpose. Initially he attempted to use C++, but soon abandoned C++ and began the creation of a new language he dubbed Oak.

Gosling decided that he still wanted to base his language on the highly successful C++, but that he would incorporate only those features of C++ that were deemed worthwhile. The features that he eliminated from the C++ plate were multiple inheritance, automatic type conversions, the use of pointers, and C++'s memory management scheme. Although the Oak technology was intriguing, the market was not quite ready for it and Oak was put on the back-burner.

With the advent of the World Wide Web, the people at Sun put two and two together, and Oak was brought out of the mothballs and renamed Java. Sun created its browser, called HotJava, using Java. By summer 1995 Java ran on SPARC Solaris, Windows NT, Windows 95, and Linux. By fall 1995, Java beta 1 was released, and the Netscape Navigator 2.0 Browser incorporated Java. Java 1.0 was officially released in January 1996.

Supporting Object-Oriented Features

Many other languages that were originally non-O-O now support some degree of O-O features. Visual Basic has been steadily adding O-O extensions. Another move of mainstream information technology toward object-technology (OT) has been introduced by SAP, the worldwide leader of client/server-based commercial application software. With Release 4.0 of SAP R/3, SAP introduced ABAP objects. This basically means with SAP's Fortune 500 client list, OT is being brought into mainstream commercial business applications. This will in no doubt further push OT!

Why Do New Languages Keep Coming Along?

It is interesting that O-O technologies keep getting so much industry attention. If you look at the sheer numbers of people programming in O-O languages and those who are not, you would wonder why we bother with O-O languages at all.

Let's explore some of the hype surrounding Java. How much is Java really being used in critical applications? I would venture to guess that the most-used language today would be

The Evolution of Object-Oriented Languages

APPENDIX B

209

B

THE EVOLUTION OF
OBJECT-ORIENTED
LANGUAGES

COBOL. If you counted up all the lines of code in each programming language, COBOL would, most likely, reign supreme. People have been writing COBOL systems for at least 25 years, so it has a long history. Add in all the other languages that are not O-O, such as C, Basic, Fortran, RPG, and so on, and you can see that by comparison, the O-O portion of the world is very small indeed.

Even if you consider the PC (most of the legacy code mentioned in the previous paragraph is on non-PC platforms such as mainframes) the languages of choice are C, C++, Visual Basic, and so on. Throw in fourth-generation tools, and O-O languages are still in the minority (a small minority). Although you can write O-O code in C++, it is considered a hybrid language. In reality, only Smalltalk and Java are widely used pure O-O languages (ADA is used by the government, so perhaps it can be considered part of the widely used category).

Smalltalk and Java

Some people would not place Smalltalk into the widely used category. Also, remember that even though many people speak of Java as being an O-O language, the primitive data types (integers, floats, and so on) are not implemented as objects.

Prior to the release of Java, Smalltalk was making some headway in the market. Smalltalk proponents played the pure O-O language card against the C++ camp. It was true that C++, being a hybrid, tended to be somewhat unwieldy. Because of its dependence on C and the fact that it had been extended multiple times, C++ was in many ways difficult to understand and use. Thus, Smalltalk experienced a bit of a revival. In fact, Smalltalk is a very powerful development environment and has a very loyal following. Smalltalk is still a force to be reckoned with and in many ways has always fought the battle of the best technology available not winning out in the marketplace.

However, the selling point that Smalltalk was the only true, pure O-O language diminished when Java emerged. In many ways, Java was the best of both worlds. It was considered a pure O-O language, and its syntax was based on C/C++.

What Makes a State-of-the-Art Language?

So what makes up a current, state-of-the-art programming language? Java is the latest in the evolutionary cycle, but what does Java claim to provide? The initial Java white paper from Sun stated that Java was "simple, object-oriented, distributed, robust, secure, architecture neutral, portable, interpreted, high performance, multithreaded, and dynamic." That's saying a lot. Let's explore how Java attempted to back up these claims.

- Simple—As already stated, Java eliminated some of the perceived complexity of C++, such as multiple inheritance, automatic type conversions, the use of pointers, and the C++ memory management scheme.

- O-O—Whereas Smalltalk is a pure O-O, C++ is a hybrid language that supports O-O features. Interestingly, the O-O features of Java are essentially those of C++, but Java enforces the O-O paradigm.

- Distributed—The Internet and networking in general are pervasive in today's market, and Java supports TCP/IP protocols such as HTTP and FTP. Java also has native support for accessing URLs.

- Robust—Java has a very strong emphasis on preventing problems in the first place and detecting them early if they do crop up. The major difference between Java and C++ in this area is that Java does not support pointers, which prevents much of the data corruption encountered when using C++. Basically, pointers give programmers just enough rope to hang themselves.

- Secure—Because Java was developed as a language for networked and distributed environments, security was a primary concern from the start. For example, when using Java with a nontrusted applet, the applet cannot update system resources outside its process space.

Trusted Applets

When the browser can authenticate an applet, normally via a digital signature, the applet is considered a *trusted applet* and may be allowed to update certain system resources.

- Architecture neutral—Java produced bytecodes that can be run on any platform which supports a Java Virtual Machine (JVM). This means that there is no system-dependent, native code.

The Java Virtual Machine

The JVM is an interpreter that inputs Java bytecodes and turns them into platform-dependent code. In this design, the bytecodes are portable and the programmer does not have to worry about writing system-dependent code. However, interpreters often suffer from performance issues, and one of the earliest criticisms of Java related to poor performance.

The Evolution of Object-Oriented Languages

APPENDIX B

211

B

THE EVOLUTION OF
OBJECT-ORIENTED
LANGUAGES

- Portable—There are, theoretically at least, no system-dependent aspects to Java. C and C++ have a lot of system-dependent aspects embedded in them. For example, an `int` in C and C++ can be 16 bits, 32 bits, or any other size, depending on the platform. An `int` in Java is always 32 bits.

- Interpreted—Java is not compiled and linked into native code like C++. Java is compiled into bytecodes and then interpreted by the JVM. Thus, any platform that has a JVM can run Java bytecodes.

- High performance—This claim is a bit more dubious than the others. Early on, the rap against Java was that it was slow. Performance has improved; however, sometimes programmers need to write code in another language for performance reasons. For example, you may need to write a routine in C++ to write to a specific device driver and call it from your Java code. However, this breaks the Java model, so you no longer have a pure Java application.

  You can also take the Java code and use features like just-in-time compilers to transform the Java bytecodes into platform-dependent native code for efficiency purposes.

- Multithreaded—*Multithreading* allows one program to do more than one thing at a time. (This is not to be confused with multiprocessing.) Multithreading leads to more real-time responsiveness from an application. However, in many languages multithreading is very complicated. Java makes multithreading much easier to manage.

- Dynamic—Classes in Java are loaded dynamically, not linked into executables. Thus, finding runtime information is much easier. It also facilitates the loading of classes over networks.

  Java greatly benefited from the lessons learned by the designers of C++. It is easy to look at Java and marvel at its elegance, but C++ did not have Java's advantage of hindsight. In fact, one of the primary reasons that Java has gained the popularity that it has is a direct result of its lineage from C++. C and C++ programmers can use Java without having to learn a new syntax.

Conclusion

What language will be the next hot topic in the O-O arena? Of course, there is no way to predict the future. The market acceptance for Smalltalk, C++, and Java has thrust O-O development into the mainstream. Thus, there is sure to be more research in the areas of O-O technologies. Acceptance of a new language, whether O-O or not, is not a quick process. However, it will be interesting to see what new and improved language will give the current set of widely used languages a run for its money in the next 5–10 years.

References

Sun Microsystems: *The Java Language: An Overview.* URL: `java.sun.com/docs/overviews/java/java-overview-1.html`.

Khoshafian, Setrag, and Razmik Abnous: *Object Orientation.* Wiley, 1995.

Stroustrup, Bjarne: *The Design and Evolution of C++.* Addison-Wesley, 1994.

INDEX

SYMBOLS

A

Object-Oriented Training

Interested in a training class based on this book?

Visit the author's Web site to arrange an on-site training class or to license the training material:

`http://www.mwprojects.com`

Or send inquiries to `info@mwprojects.com`

Why This Training Is Important

- With the explosion of the Internet and the corresponding e-commerce craze, companies must embrace object-oriented technologies just to keep up with the competition.

- While most companies are aggressively pursuing professionals with object-oriented skills, there is a severe shortage of available talent. This shortage is significantly exacerbated by the shift from Y2K projects to new e-commerce initiatives.

- The bottom line is that it is very cost effective and strategic for companies to educate their current employees in object-oriented technologies.

- One of the major mistakes that many companies make when moving to object-oriented technologies is to jump head-first into development without first understanding the object-oriented thought process.

- While the term "paradigm shift" is often overused, there is no doubt that moving to object-oriented technologies requires a major paradigm shift. Starting the shift to object-oriented technologies should not begin by learning an object-oriented language or modeling tool.

- The first order of business should be to learn the fundamental object-oriented concepts.